THE PRACTICE OF CONTEMPLATION ACCORDING TO JOHN OF THE CROSS

JAMES W. KINN.

ICS Publications
Institute of Carmelite Studies
Washington, DC

ICS Publications
2131 Lincoln Road, NE
Washington, DC 20002-1199

www.icspublications.org

Typeset and produced in the United States of America

Library of Congress Cataloging in Publication Data

Kinn, James W., 1931-
    The practice of contemplation according to John of the Cross / James W.
  Kinn.
      p. cm.
  Includes bibliographical references.
  ISBN 978-0-935216-49-3
  1. John of the Cross, Saint, 1542-1591. 2. Contemplation. I. Title.
  BX4700.J7K56 2009
  248.3'4--dc22

                                    2009013745

Contents

ACKNOWLEDGMENT REGARDING
THE SCRIPTURE QUOTES

Chapter 1
Understanding John of the Cross

The entire focus of this book will be on the practice of contemplation according to the teaching of St. John of the Cross. There are two reasons why such a study is most needed in this twenty-first century. The first reason is that contemplation has been kept under a cloud in our Catholic Church for over 300 years, as Thomas Keating observes:

> Quietism...was condemned in 1687 as a species of false mysticism by [Pope] Innocent XII....[Later] Bishop Bossuet...succeeded in having [Semi-quietism] condemned in France...; the controversy brought traditional mysticism into **disrepute.** From then on, the reading about mysticism was frowned upon in seminaries and religious communities....[As a result] the unexpurgated text of [John of the Cross'] writings appeared only in our own century, four hundred years after its writing.[1]

For more than three centuries, the church was suspicious of all forms of contemplative prayer. No mystical writing of significance was published in the eighteenth and nineteenth centuries. Even certain passages of John of the Cross were omitted from publication out of fear of condemnation. Only in the late twentieth century was the unexpurgated text of his writings finally published. Only now in this century, have the teachings of John of the Cross, Teresa of Avila and other classical writers taken their rightful place in our church and our spirituality.

The second reason for an in-depth study of John of the Cross'

---

1   Thomas Keating, *Open Mind, Open Heart* (Rockport, MA: Element Inc. 1986), pp.23-24 (emphasis added).

1

teaching on contemplation has to do with the person and style of writing of John of the Cross himself. John is rightly called the Mystical Doctor because he is without parallel in the rich content and brilliance of his teaching. His writings are profound and original. However, he is not a great stylist. His writings include tedious repetitions, disproportion of emphases, displacement of material, unwieldy sentences, and imprecise language.

Accordingly, it is no easy task to make sense of John's writing. In order for us to clearly understand him, I will try to follow some norms of clarification. The first and most important guide for understanding John of the Cross is to be always faithful to the particular **night** to which he refers. The different nights refer to various stages of prayer; such as meditation, contemplation or advanced contemplation. Often, writers who interpret John fail to indicate which night or stage he is talking about and so they confuse rather than clarify. So whenever John speaks of "this night" or "the first night," I will clarify just which night he means by considering the context.

Second, John uses terms such as "spiritual faculties, natural faculties of the body or soul, natural affections and senses of the body" which are not immediately clear to us. Sometimes he uses several terms interchangeably; in his mind they are the same or almost the same. So I will describe all these terms in the appendix; this simple table, called "Identities in John of the Cross," will explain the meaning of these terms.

The primary focus of this book will be John of the Cross' teaching on **the beginning of contemplation.** John treats the active dark nights of sense and spirit in the *Ascent of Mount Carmel, Books I, II, and III.* Some of his teaching in those three volumes deals with simple prayer and the preparation for contemplation, which I will quote when appropriate. John's main treatment of the **passive** dark nights of sense and spirit and the beginning of contemplation is found in the *Dark*

Night, Books I and II. Most of our quotes will be from these two works that concentrate on this stage of beginning contemplation. Further specific teaching about early contemplation is found in stanzas 6 to 12 of the *Spiritual Canticle* as well as in stanza III, paragraphs 30 to 62 in the *Living Flame.* Most of the references and quotes will be from these works because they concentrate on this stage of prayer. Outside of these works, John only rarely makes specific comments about the beginning of contemplation. If I quote those works, I will be careful to choose only those passages that relate to the beginning of contemplation. By limiting our focus in this way, we will avoid mixing the different stages of prayer and confusing John's teaching.

Let me now offer an overview of all the writings of John of the Cross. John, like almost all the classical spiritual writers, follows the threefold division of spirituality into the purgative, the illuminative and the unitive ways. His clearest description is found in the beginning of the *Spiritual Canticle:*

> The initial stanzas [of The Spiritual Canticle] treat of the state of beginners, that of the purgative way. The subsequent ones deal with the state of proficients...that is, of the illuminative way. The stanzas following these refer to the unitive way, that of the perfect....[2]

Admittedly, John defines these three states differently than other writers; for example, he includes contemplative prayer as a part of the illuminative way. Secondly, John is also faithful to the clear distinction into active and passive stages of prayer and spiritual life. His most complete description of the active and passive stages of prayer is found at the beginning of his *Ascent to Mount Carmel*:

---

2   SC, argument before stanza 1.

This first [night or active] purgation...which will be under discussion in...this [first] book [of the *Ascent of Mount Carmel*], concerns the sensory part of the   soul. The second [active] night...concerns the spiritual part. We shall deal with this second night, insofar as it is active, in the second and third...book[s]. In the fourth [book, which actually includes the first and second books of the *Dark Night*], we will discuss the night insofar as it is passive.[3]

To say this another way: the active night of sense and the active night of spirit are John's way of describing our active efforts at purgation of the senses and meditation; he treats this especially in the *Ascent of Mount Carmel, Book I* (sense) and *Books II and III* (spirit). Also, the passive night of sense and passive night of spirit are John's way of describing the stages of contemplation and God's supernatural action; he treats these especially in the *Dark Night, Book I* (sense) and *Book II* (spirit). He explains further: "Souls begin to enter this [passive] dark night when God draws them out of the state of beginners (those who practice meditation...), [and] begins to place them in the state of proficients (those who are already contemplatives)....[4]

---

3   A, I, 1, 2.
4   DN, I, 1, 1.

General Outline of All the Works of John of the Cross

NOTE: a word about the references to John's works that we will use throughout. All references to the works of St. John of the Cross will be taken from The Collected Works of John of the Cross, trans. Kieran Kavenaugh O. C. D. and Otilio Rodriguez O. C. D. (Washington DC: Institute of Carmelite Studies, 1979). And the individual references will follow this format: A = *Ascent of Mount Carmel, books I, II, or III.*

DN = *Dark Night, books I or II.* SC = *Spiritual Canticle*, second redaction.

LF = *Living Flame of Love*, second redaction.

A. The Way of Beginners: The Purgative Way; the Active Night

John of the Cross identifies beginners with those who meditate, with those who work actively to purify their souls, who are in the purgative way.[5] This first stage of the spiritual life is called an active night; it has two parts: 1) the active night of senses (treated especially in the *Ascent of Mount Carmel, Book I*; 2) the active night of the spirit (treated especially in the *Ascent of Mount Carmel, Books II and III*. Both of these active nights make up the purgative way.

1. The Active Night of Sense

This active night of sense is what most spiritual writers refer to as the purgative way. It consists of curtailing sins and attachments, slowly renouncing sinful pleasures and self-centered gratification. John calls this a **night** because just as dark night deprives our eyes of sight, so this discipline deprives all our sense of (disorderly) activity. He calls

---

5   DN, I, 1, 1.

it **active** because it involves our deliberate action of such denial and restraint. And he calls it the night of **sense** because it involves primarily the passions and pleasures of sense.[6]

The primary effort in this active night of sense is to renounce every pleasure and satisfaction that is not in the service of God.[7] This active night is part of the celebrated teaching on the NADA (nothing) and TODO (everything). NADA doesn't mean doing away with all natural pleasures or possessions but rather all disordered desire or **attachment** for them.[8] For, once we free ourselves from the unruly desire for pleasures and possessions (NADA), then we can find delight in everything (TODO).

2. The Active Night of Spirit

The active night of spirit deals essentially with the active progress from common meditation to a simple prayer of faith. People who practice meditation generally begin with some form of sense images, ideas, affections and reasoning. Quite naturally, over time, such prayer tends to grow into a more simple prayer that is less and less active, less filled with repeated ideas and images. Their prayer tends to grow into a simple act of faith. At this point they often wonder what they are doing wrong, what happened to their satisfying prayer, why their prayer is so dark. John of the Cross would shout loudly that nothing is wrong, everything is developing naturally and the darkness is only a sign of progress.

---

6   A fine description of the two active nights (as well as the two passive nights) is found in Ross Collins, *John of the Cross* (Collegeville, MN: The Liturgical Press, 1990), pp. 63-73.

7   A, I, 13, 4.

8   A, I, 3, 4: "…we are not discussion the mere lack of things…. We are dealing with the denudation of the soul's **appetites**… that is, what leaves it free and empty of all things, even though it possesses them." Seealso: Thomas Dubay, *The Fire Within* (San Francisco: Ignatius Press, 1989), p. 142.

John calls this stage a **night** because it is a deliberate refraining from the pursuit of sensible consolations; it cultivates interior silence. It is an **active** night because it involves deliberately subduing ideas and images in prayer. It is a night of **spirit** for it involves setting the soul at rest in mental prayer; it is a simple act of faith and attentiveness to God.

B. The Way of Proficients; the Illuminative Way; the Passive Night.

John of the Cross identifies proficients with contemplatives who are in the illumina-tive way.[9] This second stage of the spiritual life is called a passive night and it has two parts: 1) the passive night of sense (treated especially in the *Dark Night, Book I*); 2) the passive night of the spirit (treated especially in the *Dark Night, Book II*).

1. The Passive Night of Sense

This passive night of sense is God's way of purifying the soul. It consists of a lack of pleasure or consolation in prayer and in life. John explains in absolute terms: "…these souls do not get satisfaction or consolation from the things of God, they do not get any out of creatures either…in order to dry up and purge its sensory appetite. He does not allow it to find sweetness or delight in anything."[10] John calls this a **night** because it is filled with darkness and aridity; God brings the soul into darkness and emptiness in prayer and life. It is **passive** because it is caused by God's action in the soul; there is an inability to actively meditate. It is a passive night of **sense,** because it is without any consolation or affection. The primary work is God's, freeing us from a dependence on sensible satisfaction in prayer and restraining our sense desires. This work of God is essential for progress in prayer; we cannot accomplish this purification by ourselves. This state is

---

9   DN, I, 1, 1 and SC, theme before stanza 1.

10   DN, I, 9, 2.

already the beginning of contemplation, but not so that we can clearly experience it.[11]

2. The Passive Night of Spirit

John describes this night as a sense of powerlessness and radical poverty of spirit in prayer. He calls it a **night** because it is a dark and loving gaze of faith; it is contemplation or the hidden inflow of God in the soul.[12] It is **passive** because it is strictly God's doing not the result of our action. It is a night of **spirit** because it is an obscure encounter with God in prayer.

C. The Way of the Perfect; the Unitive Way; Divine Union

At he end of the *Dark Night, Book II*, John comments on the verse, "My house being now at rest":

> ...I went out to divine union with God through love. Insofar as, the soul is...purged through the war of the dark night in a twofold way (in the sensory and spiritual parts with their senses, faculties, and passions), it also attains a twofold peace and quiet....[13]

But his actual teaching on the unitive way is developed especially in his other two major works: *Spiritual Canticle,*[14] and *Living Flame of Love.*[15] The connection between the *Dark Night* and these other books is expressed well in the *Living Flame*:

---

11   DN, I, 9, 6: "...[this arid state] is the beginning of a contemplation that is dark and dry to the senses. Ordinarily this contemplation...is secret and hidden from the very one who receives it."

12   DN, II, 5, 1.

13   DN, II, 24, 1-2.

14   SC, 23, 3.

15   LF, prologue, 3-4.

In the Dark Night…we dealt with the intensity of this purgation… of the sensory part and…of the spiritual part, and the time or stage along the spiritual road in which it begins…. Let it suffice [now] to know that the very God who [seeks]…the transformation of love is he who first assails and purges it….[16]

This unitive way is the supernatural work of the Holy Spirit, which enkindles a flame of love in the soul. The *Living Flame* begins with the first line of the poem: "O living flame of love" and is clearly explained by John: "This flame of love is the Spirit of its Bridegroom, which is the Holy Spirit…. Such is the activity of the Holy Spirit in the soul transformed in love…."[17]

The term John uses for this transformation in the unitive way is "spiritual marriage."

In the introduction (and again in stanza 22), John presents a fine outline of the **Spiritual Canticle** and again shows that his whole spirituality follows the classical division of three stages of the spiritual life:

A. Purgative Way: stanzas 1-5
B. Illuminative Way:
    1. Dark contemplation: stanzas 6-12
    2. Espousal (the goal of the illuminative way): stanzas 13-21
C. Unitive Way:
    1. Spiritual marriage: stanzas 22-35
    2. Beatific state: stanzas 36-40.

We can conclude, then, that John of the Cross's spiritual teaching is generally in keeping with this threefold division of the spiritual life as taught by the classical spiritual writers of our rich Catholic tradition.

---

16   LF, I, 25.
17   *Idem.* 3.

However his second division, that of the illuminative way, is more advanced, for it starts with the beginning of contemplation. Thus, John uses the term, beginners, for those who are just starting out in meditation or practicing more simple prayer; he uses the term, progressives, for those who are experiencing the beginning of contemplation; and he applies the term, perfect, to those in the unitive way.

Chapter 2
Our Experience of Prayer

Let me begin with the common experience of prayer – which may reflect your experience too. The most common experience of people who were serious about prayer and meditation at some time in their life was something like the following. We began to learn about mediation early in the seminary or religious life or in some prayerful Christian community. No matter what form of spirituality and prayer we learned, we were first taught a solid form of meditation; it may have included an introduction (preludes), a reflection on scripture or the life of Jesus (points), a personal reaction (faith, affections), and a conclusion (final prayer or resolution).

This form of prayer was practiced for some years with varying degrees of success. Little by little our prayer became less intellectual or theological and more personal and affective. Sometimes we felt more devotional; our feelings became warmer and stronger; prayer was often a delight to us; Jesus was our personal friend and model; we were attracted to him more and more; we were in love with our gentle Savior.

In time our prayer slowed down and simplified. We didn't find many new ideas to occupy our intellect and our emotions quieted down. We felt no need to be busy about many things, like Martha, but were content to sit at the feet of Jesus, like Mary. It seemed very natural that our prayer should grow more and more simple. Though we were not so active, we experienced a deeper intimacy with our Lord. We still felt we were making progress and experienced a feeling of comfort and confidence. But then many of us experienced a crisis in our prayer life; in time our prayer became so simple that it almost disappeared. Not only were we without engaging ideas to occupy us or spontaneous

11

affections to hearten us, there was not even a sense of sitting at the feet of Jesus in simple love. There was no clarity of thought, distinctness of image, nor sensible fervor. And so the crisis grew -- with a heavy sense of weariness and distaste for mental prayer. We felt frustrated and confused because we seemed to be getting nowhere; our prayer life seemed to fade away; we began to sense that our interior life had reached a dead end.

Let me describe what I did at this point, as one example. I continued to pray anyway, even though my prayer got more dry and more dark. I found various alternative forms of simple meditation: reflection on a scripture passage or an enlightening section in a spiritual book, or even centering prayer. But nothing really improved the situation. It became so painful to pray that I would find excuses to avoid prayer, or I would continue to spend the time only because I thought empty prayer was better than no prayer at all, and some kind of prayer was essential for union with Christ.

Others who were faithful to prayer had different experiences. Some of us tried every form of meditation we came in contact with, whether it was yoga, *lectio divina*, praying with music and incense, praying outdoors with so-called creation prayer, centering prayer, praying with a sacred word or mantra, or the prayer of presence. Whatever seemed to give us some personal contact with Jesus was our prayer of choice.

Still others just gave up regular mental prayer. We told ourselves that our ministry to God's people was a way to experience God each day. Or if we were priests, we thought that our life was so full with masses, weddings, funerals, baptisms, and prayer services that there was no time or need for meditation.

Didn't one or other of these experiences come to many of us? Didn't we make these adjustments over the years – either with great deliberation and care, or with just an imperceptible drifting into such a way of life? It was not that we were totally irresponsible or foolish. Quite the contrary. But what we didn't know was, that there was another way. We didn't understand that when our prayer got more and more simple and dark, we were not up against a wall but in front of a door – a door that we never imagined. What we were experiencing in our prayer was not a dead end but a way forward. What no one told us was that our prayer was developing naturally and positively. What we needed was an experienced guide to show us the road ahead. If only we had someone to explain that, though it was a dark road, it was a wonderful next step to drawing close to Jesus. We had no one to encourage us to go forward on this road rather than take some side roads.

Enter John of the Cross! What he says to us is that this experience, that so many of us went through, is entirely natural – following the usual way of simplification of prayer. The place where we have come to is an integral part of the development of prayer; and what we now experience is a necessary stage of our progress in prayer – without it we could not go farther. All of this John of the Cross can teach us:

> Perhaps the greatest debt that Christianity owes to John of the Cross is for the clarity with which he showed that the Dark Night of the Soul was not a dead loss in the spiritual life...but was an **integral part** of the development of prayer.[1]

This is the key to John's teaching about the beginning of contemplation. That is, we come to contemplation not by greater clarity of our natural powers of understanding, but by slowly opening ourselves to the tenuous, obscure, new kind of knowledge of God; we come not by struggling harder to pray but by calmly remaining quiet

---

1   Leonard Boase, S.J., *The Prayer of Faith* (Chicago: Loyola Press, 1985), p. 78 (emphasis added).

before God; we come by learning that this new form of prayer is God's work alone, not our effort at all. The image is not one of knocking down a wall but of confidently waiting for a door to open; the state is not that of one who comes to the end of the road but of one who is being made ready to be transported on a wonderful journey.

SUGGESTION FOR PRAYER

NOTE: At the end of each chapter I will add a suggestion for the beginning of prayer or some helpful encouragement for prayer. I will try to make such recommendations appropriate for that chapter and stage of prayer. Sometimes a scripture passage and comment may offer an insight. Sometimes I will offer guidelines or insights into John's method of contemplation. Here, at the end of this chapter, is a suggested prayer.

Lord God, Paul teaches us to pray as your son/daughter. We know that we are your children because we have the Spirit of your own son in our hearts who cries out "*Abba,* Father." How can you not hear your children? How can you not hear your Holy Spirit who "intercedes for [us] according to God's will" (Rom. 8, 27)? How can you not hear us who echo the cry of Jesus himself, "*Abba,* Father?" You, Lord, have shown us the whole truth in your Son. You have no other wisdom or revelation to give us than Jesus, who is your Word. I look for no other answers, no other expression of who you are, no other truth to believe than Jesus. To see the Son is to see you, the Father; to know him is to know you; to believe in him is to gain eternal life with you.

Chapter 3
Simple Prayer of Faith

St. John of the Cross treats the active night of the spirit in books
II and III of the *Ascent of Mount Carmel*. He describes this second of
the active nights this way:

> ...the first [active] night...pertains to the lower sensory part of
> man's nature....The second [active] darker night of faith, belongs
> to the rational, superior part; it is darker and more interior because
> it deprives this part of its rational light, or better, blinds it.[1]

Repeatedly John identifies this active night of the spirit with
pure faith that is very dark, because it receives no help from the senses
or from the understanding:

> ...this spiritual night of faith removes everything, both in the
> intellect and in the senses. As a result the soul declares...that it
> departed in darkness and secure. For the less a soul works with its
> own abilities, the more securely it proceeds, because its progress
> in faith is greater.[2]

The active night of the spirit deals essentially with the active
progress from common meditation to a simple prayer of faith. That
is, our prayer at this stage becomes naturally more simple, with less
and less intellectual work or affective response. Then prayer tends to
grow into a simple act of faith. At this point we wonder what we are

---

1   A, II, 2, 2.
2   *Ibid.* 1, 3.

doing wrong, what happened to our satisfying prayer, why our prayer is so dark. John of the Cross wants us to know that **nothing** is wrong, everything is developing naturally, and the darkness is actually a sign of progress.

John tells us quite simply that in this stage of prayer it is wrong for us to struggle for the sensible thoughts, images, affections and reasonings of meditation:

> They strive hard to meditate, but draw out little satisfaction, or none at all; rather their lot becomes aridity, fatigue and restlessness of soul. This aridity augments as their strivings through meditation for that former sweetness ...increase. [They do not need this food but] another food, more delicate...by pacifying the soul, by leaving it to its more spiritual quiet and repose.[3]

But how are we to know that we have come to that point in our prayer life when we are to cease meditating in the accustomed way and begin to practice this simple prayer of faith? John gives us three famous signs for knowing that it is **time for us to leave discursive meditation:**

> The first [sign] is the realization that one cannot make discursive meditation nor receive satisfaction from it as before. The second sign is an awareness of a disinclination to fix the imagination or sense faculties upon other particular objects, exterior or interior. The third and surest sign is that a person likes to remain alone in loving awareness of God, without particular considerations, in interior peace and repose...in a general, loving awareness and knowledge....[4]

---

3   *Ibid.* 12, 6.

4   *Ibid.* 13, 2-4.

Let me try to express John's reasoning here. The first sign implies that we have received all the spiritual profit we can by meditation and reasoning. Consider, for example, how we learn to write correct English. Once we have learned the basic rules of punctuation and grammar, we center all our efforts on more advanced matters, such as unity, coherence and style. Something similar is true of our learning to pray. After we have spent years in imagining, reasoning, and affectively responding to all the rational parts of our faith, we are ready for more advanced prayer – just being with God in a simple prayer of faith. This simple prayer of faith itself prepares us for a completely new way of knowing him – the way of infused contemplation. Or look at this another way, by adding the second sign. When discursive meditation has become practically impossible, it becomes harmful for us to force our mind to have precise thoughts and our will to express affections it does not feel; that is a sign that we should move on to this next and natural stage. The third sign describes our prayer at this transitional stage as the only alternative open to us; that is, we have necessarily given up discursive meditation and have not yet arrived at infused contemplation; so the only kind of helpful prayer is this simple prayer of faith. We must have courage to suspend our own thoughts, imaginations and reasonings, and wait with confidence for God to show himself to us in a new way. This gift of God's presence comes gradually, according to our success at closing down our own reflections and being more open and prepared for God's infused grace. Our prayer remains suspended between the past activity that no longer has a reason to exist, and a future activity which has not happened yet – namely, God's showing himself to us directly in contemplation.

What can we do during this time of waiting? How should we pray? This is the most critical question for us, for this is the stage of prayer that seems to be a dead-end wall rather than a door to contemplation. The rest of this chapter will try to answer this question practically, at great length.

John himself expresses this question for us:

> A question may arise: [whether those who are in this stage of prayer must] never again practice discursive meditation.... We did not mean that those beginning to have this general loving knowledge should never again try to meditate. In the beginning of this state the habit of contemplation is not so perfect that one can, at will, enter into this act, neither is one so remote from discursive meditation as to be always incapable of it.[5]

We need to be very clear about this answer. At this stage of prayer, John's answer is quite similar to Teresa of Avila's counsel in her *Interior Castle*.[6] Both of these doctors of mystical theology assure us that when we are not yet experiencing contemplation regularly but can at times meditate discursively, we should do that freely. John of the Cross will give a different answer (urging us never to go back to regular discursive meditation) once we reach the passive night of sense and actual infused contemplation. We will carefully take note of his different response when we treat that section.

Perhaps here, more than at any stage of our progress in prayer, do we need endless encouragement. We seem to be getting nowhere in prayer; we feel dry and without consolation; we feel helpless and alone, useless and empty; we see the insufficiency of our most dedicated efforts at prayer. What consolation do John of the Cross and others offer us here?

---

5   *Ibid.*15, 1.

6   Teresa of Avila, *The Interior Castle* (Westminster, Maryland: The Newman Press, 1945), fourth mansion, chapter 3, pp. 36-39.

First, they would assure us again, that this simple prayer of faith is an integral part of the development of prayer; it is natural and necessary. Second, they remind us that it is the only way we can be prepared for the rest of the journey. We must first become deaf, blind, mute, empty and helpless in terms of all our natural faculties; only then will we be perfectly open and receptive to the transforming grace of God. As long as we feel strong, wise and effective with our natural abilities in prayer, we will not feel the need to turn to God for his help. Third, they explain that the negative component of this experience (the failure of our reason and will) is connected to the positive component (the new action of God and his immediate presence); the negative one appears only that the positive one may grow and grow. Fourth, they point to where we are going, so that we can at least rationally see the light at the end of the tunnel. That is, though now his presence is imperceptible to us – more like an absence – in time, his new presence will increase slowly and tenuously; occasionally and briefly, he will show himself as a gleam in the night; eventually this presence will seem to surge up from the depths of our being.

Finally, they point to the one virtue that is so necessary here – as it is in our whole following of Jesus: total trust in God. This total trust in God in prayer is our source of power in the active night of the spirit. Our fundamental stance before God is one of poverty of spirit in all of the spiritual life; that is, we cannot depend on anything of our own – not our efforts, merits, or good works; we are simply nothing, empty, dependent before God. Only this poverty of spirit makes us totally open and receptive to God's grace. John insists that once the soul does its part by becoming poor in spirit, God will certainly do his part by infusing his grace of contemplation:

...[Lk. 14, 33: "[E]veryone of you who does not renounce all his possessions cannot be my disciple"] refers not only to the renunciation...of all corporal and temporal things, but also to the dispossession of spiritual things which includes spiritual poverty, to which the Son of God ascribes beatitude [Mk. 5, 3]. When the soul...attains to emptiness and dispossession [of all things], it is impossible that God fail to do his part by communicating himself to it, at least silently and secretly.[7]

Here John applies this poverty of spirit particularly to our life of prayer; he explains that this poverty of spirit means accepting the emptiness and darkness of all our faculties in prayer, so that we can only wait for God's action and his gift of infused prayer. He identifies this spirit of poverty with darkness, emptiness and detachment.[8] Regarding prayer then, this means that we come to emptiness, darkness and powerlessness, first by our own efforts (as here in the active night of the spirit), and later by God's extraordinary grace (in the passive night).

We need to be very honest in describing this experience. Increasingly, the experience is one of being suspended in a no-man's land; we can no longer pray in the old way of meditation and simple prayer, while at the same time we have not yet reached the new form of

---

7   LF, III, 46. This is the first time we have quoted from the *Living Flame.* Most of this book deals with the **unitive way,** which is beyond our focus for this book. But paragraphs 30-62 of stanza III deal precisely with those who are **beginning contemplation.** Throughout this section (30-62), John of the Cross is instructing spiritual directors how to help those who are beginning to practice contemplation, when "God begins to wean the soul...and place it in the state of contemplation." He cautions: "Therefore, directors should not impose meditation upon persons in this state.... Such activity would place an obstacle in the path of the principal agent Who...is God.... Thus the individual should proceed only with a loving attention to God, without making specific acts. He should conduct himself passively...with a simple, loving awareness..."(32-33). Note that almost all our quotes from the *Living Flame* will be from this section (30-62).

8   A, II, 24, 8.

prayer, i. e., contemplation. The actual experience will vary; sometimes we will receive some light or comfort; but commonly our prayer will be dark and arid. When such is our actual experience, we understand that we must suspend our own activities, stop weaving our own ideas, cease squeezing out affections. But that leaves us with a void of our own activity, without an immediate response from God.

Over a period of time this aridity increases, and our tolerance of such prayer of pure faith almost vanishes. Our prayer becomes more and more dry and irksome; we feel repelled by the very thought of spending time in such prayer. We feel mute, deaf, numb and empty before a God who is hidden and seems absent. At times we reach such a degree of impotence and insensibility that we seem to have become like stones frozen in a glacier.

What are we to do? John answers simply:

> [The soul's only food consists] in pacifying the soul, by leaving it to its more spiritual quiet and repose. The more spiritual a man is, the more he discontinues trying to make particular acts with his faculties, for he becomes more engrossed in one general pure act.[9]

That is, we must persevere patiently in prayer in a simple attentiveness to God, without trying to force ourselves to say, do, or feel anything. Our only effort is to remain at rest and quiet; we do little more than wait and endure.

This experience is called the active night of the spirit. In what way is it **active**? It is active only as **attentiveness;** it is a single act of faith; it is a general and loving realization of God's presence. Yet this general realization is at times so subtle and delicate that we cannot perceive it, even though we are occupied in it. There is also another sense in which

---

9   *Ibid.* 12, 6.

this night is active. It is active in the negative sense, i.e., inasmuch as we **deliberately refrain** from sensible images, rational thoughts and affections; we freely commit ourselves to this inner austerity of prayer, which is the only way to reach God in a new way of prayer.

The number one problem for us in this stage is the sense that we are doing nothing, that we are getting nowhere; we understand nothing distinctly, and so we feel we cannot be making progress! John answers this wrenching cry most sensitively:

> I reply that, quite the contrary, if it would have particular knowledge, it would not advance. The reason is that God transcends the intellect and is incomprehensible and inaccessible to it.... Hence while the intellect is understanding, it is not approaching God but withdrawing from Him. It must withdraw from itself and from its knowledge so as to journey to God in faith, by believing and not understanding.[10]

That is, only when we void our mind of rational thoughts and images can we have room for a new and direct knowledge of God. John continues the same argument with regard to the memory and the will; for example: "by not turning back in the embrace of something sensible, it goes forward to the inaccessible, which is God."[11]

All this helps to explain John's famous paradoxes in his "Sketch of Mount Carmel:" "To come to the knowledge of all, desire the knowledge of nothing. To reach satisfaction in all, desire its possession in nothing."[12] Why is this actually going forward? Because it is a

---

10   LF. III, 48. Notice the explanation found above in footnote 7.

11   *Ibid.* 51.

12   See the "Sketch of Mount Carmel" found at the beginning of the *Ascent of Mount Carmel,* Kavanaugh, p. 67.

preparation for the journey. Because remaining in quiet and tranquility, without struggling for thoughts and ideas, results "in purity of...soul, which is a greater benefit...[for that disposes the soul] excellently for human and divine wisdom."[13] Thus remaining quietly recollected, and not disturbed with all kinds of desires and affections, is a fine preparation for being moved on another level by the Holy Spirit.

To say this another way: to seek what we think is fulfillment by our natural efforts is to lose our way. We must be brought to emptiness and powerlessness, or we would constantly be falling back on our own feeble reasonings. We must allow God to bring us to his fulfillment by the eventual infusion of the light of the Holy Spirit. And in this transitional stage we must be content with preparing for the journey and not bemoan the fact that we have to wait in emptiness and faith.

In the last fifty years or so other forms of prayer have become very popular that are similar to this simple prayer of faith. They can be most effective ways of praying in this transitional state between ordinary meditation and contemplation. One method is that of centering prayer. This consists of a very simple attentiveness to God in a peaceful, quiet waiting. It uses a sacred word that we ourselves choose, such as "Jesus" or "Spirit," that is often repeated in order to keep our mind open and receptive to God. This form of prayer is championed by several spiritual writers today. Thomas Keating explains centering prayer very engagingly in his *Open Mind, Open Heart*.[14]

A similar form of prayer is the prayer of presence. An excellent description of this form of prayer is found in *Practicing the Prayer of Presence* by Susan Muto and Adrian van Kaam.[15] This form of prayer

---

13 A, III, 6, 1.

14 Thomas Keating, *Open Mind, Open Heart,* especially chapters 5 and 10.

15 Adrian van Kaam and Susan Muto, *Practicing the Prayer of Presence* (Mineola, NY: Resurrection Press, 1993), especially book one, section 4, pp. 47-57.

consists mainly of two attitudes: watching and waiting. That is, we simply wait for God's presence, even in darkness, trusting that God will reveal himself in his good time.

SUGGESTION FOR PRAYER

Here is one suggestion of simple prayer based on Jesus' word of encouragement in Luke's Gospel:

"[A]sk and you will receive; seek and you will find; knock and the door will be opened to you. For everyone who asks, receives; and the one who seeks, finds; and to the one who knocks, the door will be opened.... [H]ow much more will the Father in heaven give the holy Spirit to those who ask him?" (Lk. 11, 9-13)

Lord, you yourself teach me to be confident and persevering in prayer; you give this universal law: God will hear you when you pray. Most of all, you promise to give the Holy Spirit as our guide in doing your will. You do not say when you will open the door; and you do not promise satisfaction and light; but you do promise that you will do this. I trust in your promise and your Spirit.

Receive, O Lord, my whole spirit; receive my body and senses as they are silent and dark; receive my affections as they are empty; receive my memory as it is frozen; receive my intellect in its blindness; receive my will incapable of action. Whatever I have and possess I have from you. And now all these faculties are helpless and dark. Yet this darkness is my friend, for only in the dark can your faint light be seen; this silence is the way to wisdom, for only in quiet and lack of noise can your gentle voice be heard; this emptiness is receptive, for the more I see this void in my heart, the more you prepare me to fill it; this weakness is my strength, for only when I know that I am nothing and you are God, will you give your power; this helplessness is my potency, for unless I know my inability, you will not help in a new way; inactivity is my transport, for I cannot come to your light, but must be carried by you; nothingness is my goal, for that is where new being and life begin. Give me only your Spirit of wisdom and love. Then I am rich enough; nor do I desire anything else.

* * * * *

All of this is meant to be simply a standing before God in quiet and openness. If some simple meditation develops, we can go with it. But this dark receptivity is itself a profound prayer and usually the only kind of prayer God wants of us now. Whenever our mind wanders, we can center it again by use of a sacred word, such as "Jesus" or "Spirit". Most of our prayer time can be spent in this dark, empty receptivity.

This is the only effective way for us to realize that we are completely blind, deaf, mute, cold, helpless. This sense of void is the immediate preparation for God to fill us in a way he never could, if we still depended on our own natural faculties and reasoning. The greater our hunger, thirst and emptiness, the more we can turn to God in trust: "How much more will the Father in heaven give the holy Spirit to those who ask him."

Chapter 4
Providence and Human Freedom

So much of what was said in the last two chapters describes not only our own activity but also God's grace and influence in our prayer. In the coming chapters, we will speak of the **passive** night of sense, including trials "sent" by God as well as God's infusion of contemplative prayer. Much of the terminology that John of the Cross uses, together with our similar comments, would lead us to question just how free we are and just how much is the direct action of God. In order to offer some clarity about God's providence active in our lives and our own human freedom, we need to discuss this question here.

Two important theological issues that the Catholic Church has never defined are: 1) grace, just how it works with freewill and 2) providence, how God influences nature and human activities. In fact, despite the rancorous debates by theologians over centuries, the church refused to settle such issues and simply put an end to the contentious arguments. When we read John of the Cross, we can easily be confused about the influence of God's grace and providence, especially when we consider God's work in our world and in contemplation. So, let me describe my sense of God's providence in our world and then try to understand what John teaches about God's influence in our ordinary spiritual life as well as God's direct action in contemplation.

First, how does God's providence affect our world now? This question has become very prominent in our world, because of several great tragedies in the last few years: tsunamis, earthquakes, flood, and epidemics. "Where is God in the tsunami?" ask the media. If God rules this world of ours, how could God permit the death of so many innocent people? We must admit that neither Scripture nor our church gives a single, consistent answer to such questions. In the Hebrew Scriptures (the Old Testament), God was seen as the cause of every-thing – all that was good and all that was bad. So the scripture writers agonized over the question, "If God is all just, how can bad things happen to good people?" They never really solved this question.

But in the New Testament, Christ gave a much clearer answer. At one point, Jesus was walking with a crowd of people, when he saw a man who was blind from birth. His disciples asked him, "'[W]ho sinned, this man or his parents, that he was born blind?' Jesus answered, 'Neither he nor his parents sinned; it is so that the works of God might be made visible through him'" (Jo. 9, 3). Twice in Luke, Jesus presents a similar question and answers in the same way: "Do you think that because these Galileans suffered in this way they were greater sinners than all the other Galileans? By no means!"(Lk. 13, 2-5). That is, Jesus consistently teaches that there is no causal con-nection between natural tragedies and God's punishment, between God's action and human guilt. We have to conclude that in this life there is no direct connection between natural tragedies and God's direct action.

Let me say this another way. All things in this world – all human beings and all of nature – are created by God. So the **ultimate cause** of everything is God, our creator. But human beings are really free, so that they are the immediate and direct causes of human actions. And natural phenomena occur according to the laws of nature. So the **immediate cause** of all human actions and of all natural occurrences is human or natural. Therefore, the answer to every question about why anything happens – including the great human and natural trag-edies of life – is human or natural. God is simply not in the tsunami, the earthquake, the human evil acts or tragedies. God is not the direct cause of any of these. The only note I might add is that we Christians leave room for miracles and for God's material answer to prayers.

In order to understand this common problem more completely, we need to concentrate on the gift of human freedom. If we are really free human beings, then we are not marionettes on a string, manipulated by God. If we are really free, then we must be able to choose to disobey God's will and do senseless, harmful, inhuman things. If we are really free, then things cannot always go our way, and life will not be consistently just and equitable. If we are really free, then human beings will not always act according to God's will. What all this implies is that God's providence **does not arrange things in our external world**. God does not make a farce of human freedom, does not interfere with the freedom he gave us. For without that freedom, we would no longer be really human. In a similar way, natural elements must act according to their necessarily imperfect nature.

But scripture also teaches that God's providence and care of us is **internal**. God's action is within our hearts and minds. That is, if we are faithful Christians, then God does have a **profound influence** on us without interfering in our freedom. Thus, because of our faith in God, we envision our entire outlook on life. In God's calling us as Christians, we freely choose, day by day, a way of living. In God's scriptural word, we are able to find our values for life. In Christ, we have a model for our living. In Jesus, we have an adequate motive for loving all people. In God we form our dreams and establish our hopes. The more faithful we are as Christians, the more our hopes and dreams can be realized in Christ. This is **the way that God provides for us**; this is the way God influences us freely and humanly. We remain entirely free; yet God instills within us, by his grace, everything we need for mature, human living. God is then the God "in [whom] we live and move and have our being" (Acts 17, 28). Through the Holy Spirit, whom we receive in our baptism, God offers us real freedom in our imperfect world, as he draws us by his love and by the example of Jesus.

Let us try to relate this to John of the Cross' teaching about God's providence in our ordinary spiritual life – in what he refers to as the **active night** of sense and the active night of spirit. Consider, first, all the ordinary trials, failures and frustration of everyday life and the occasional extraordinary sufferings that just happen to all of us. Modern spiritual writers see these ordinary human trials of everyday life as just that – **common human trials**. Generally speaking, they are not sent directly by God as particular trials chosen by God but are the result of nature acting naturally and human beings acting freely. Because we are really free, God does not manipulate us. The only **direct agents** in human events commonly are nature and human beings.

Nevertheless, all these trials that just come to us from others or from our circumstances are not chosen by us; we usually do not seek them or want them naturally. They are neither sent by God nor chosen by us. Whatever happens to us naturally, can be accepted by us through the grace of God. As St. Paul put it: "God is the one who…works in you both to desire and to work" (Phil. 2, 13).

This is how we can understand all that John teaches in the three books of the *Ascent to Mount Carmel*. That is, the active nights of sense and spirit consist mostly of the ordinary trials of human living, along with our freely chosen means of overcoming our own faults and imperfections.

To be faithful to John's method of active nights of purgation, however, we should take note of his **extreme** method of ascetic puri-fication: "Endeavor to be inclined always: not to the easiest, but to the most difficult; not to the most delightful, but to the harshest; not to the most gratifying, but to the less pleasant."[1] Note that he does not suggest always to **choose** the most difficult but to be **inclined** to it. The purpose of this counsel is to accomplish "a complete remedy for mortifying and pacifying the passions."[2] Other spiritual writers are **not so extreme** in their asceticism, but their goal is the same: to rid ourselves of all the faults and vices that hinder our following of Christ.

When John begins to describe the **passive night** of sense, he offers three famous signs for us to know that we are ready to begin contemplation. His description of these signs includes human difficulties that we find ourselves in, as our prayer develops naturally: "[T]hese souls do not get satisfaction...from the things of God.... The memory ordinarily turns to God solicitously.... [And there is a] powerlessness ...to meditate...."[3] Notice that these signs come to us naturally, as our prayer becomes more and more simple and less satisfying; to some degree they are a part of the ordinary development of prayer. Without denying God's hand in this state, it seems clear that John is certainly considering a **natural, human development of prayer**.

Can we say a similar thing about the **ordinary trials** of human living that John describes in the passive night of sense?

Ruth Burrows, in her *Guidelines for Mystical Prayer*,[4] considers "the ordinary trials which everyone must undergo" as part of God's plan but not necessarily his direct action:

> The [passive] dark nights are by and large the common lot, **the ordinary trials which everyone must undergo.**

---

1   A, I, 13, 6.

2   *Ibid.* 5.

3   DN, I, 9, 2, 3 and 8.

4   Ruth Burrows, *Guidelines for Mystical Prayer* (Denville, N. J.: Dimension Books, 1980).

These are precisely the means by which God purifies us: difficulties of temperament, ill-health, disappointments as well as the grievous suffering of human beings.... How wise [God] is, hiding his deepest action in what is utterly human.[5]

Again, without denying God's plan in all this, "the ordinary trials which everyone must undergo" are not necessarily the result of God's direct action. Nevertheless, these ordinary trials of free human living can be the means of our purification. "[W]hat is utterly human" can be accepted with God's grace and thus lead to our purification.

However, when John describes **contemplation itself**, he does teach that it involves the **direct action of God**. Again and again he insists: "the soul no longer has the power to work or meditate with the faculties on the things of God."[6] And therefore, "in this state of contemplation...it is God who works in it."[7] Throughout the *Dark Night*, the *Spiritual Canticle* and the *Living Flame,* John insists on this mystical grace that comes directly from God and is received passively by the soul. He teaches that our only action is to be open, attentive and receptive before God. In other words, contemplation involves the **direct action of God** on the soul, which is passive except for its being open and attentive to God.

REFLECTION

We can learn from the saints and from ordinary Christians to accept the trials of our everyday life – our woundedness, our limited temperaments, our psychic pains, our burn-out. They are not chosen

---

5   *Ibid.* pp. 38-39 (emphasis added).

6   DN, I, 10, 1.

7   *Ibid.* 9, 7. See also: *ibid* 10, 6: "For contemplation is nothing else than a secret and...loving inflow of God...."

by us, but by accepting them they can be part of our purification in the passive night of the senses:

> Some natures suffer very much from inner turmoils, bouts of depression and resentment, which they cannot will away.... Such afflictions are aptly linked with Paul's "thorn of the flesh" and serve the same purpose of God's design. Surely then, we can bring ourselves to accept our difficult temperaments, our psychic wounds, our shadows which cause much pain and **use them to grow in love.**[8]

Surely, we can agree with Paul that "...all things work for good for those who love God..." (Rom. 8, 28). So our suggestion here is that all the events of our everyday life, which we do not choose, can be used to purify us in this passive night.

How do the struggles of everyday bring about this purification of the senses? Failure and negative criticism tend to destroy our self-complacency; burnout and repugnance for everything can impress us with our poverty and nothingness; lack of satisfaction in our prayer and work naturally destroys our egotism; illness and suffering impress us with our weakness; disappointment and rejection remind us of our common human condition. The Letter to the Hebrews teaches the amazing truth that Christ himself became "perfect through suffering" (Heb. 2, 10); that is, the suffering, that he did not choose but came to him from others, became the means of his human perfection. For us too, all those trials, that we do not choose but do accept in the spirit of Jesus, can be the means of our purification in Christ.

---

8   Ruth Burrows, *Ascent to Love* (Denville, NJ: Dimension Books, 1987), pp. 34-35 (emphasis added).

Chapter 5
Jesus Our Model

What place does the life and person of Jesus have in the spirituality of John of the Cross? How central is the humanity of Jesus 1) to John's way of spirituality and 2) to his method of contemplation?

First, consider his way of spirituality. According to St. John of the Cross, we make progress in the spiritual life only by imitating Christ: "A man makes progress only through imitation of Christ, who is the Way, the Truth, and the Life. No one goes to the Father but through Him, as he states Himself in St. John [Jo. 14, 6]."[1] Here John of the Cross teaches that Christ is the center of our Christian life, and he appeals to this critical quote in John's Gospel.

This quote is variously interpreted by scripture exegetes. What we want to do in this chapter is understand clearly the way that John of the Cross understands these words of Christ, and then give a careful exegesis of them in John's Gospel itself.

For John of the Cross, Jesus is the way, the truth, and the life for us because he is our **model**; he is the model we are to imitate. In the quote above, John interprets these words of Jesus Christ as referring to the **imitation of Christ** and adds "I should not consider any spirituality worthwhile that would...run from the imitation of Christ."[2] Also in the very next paragraph he adds: "Christ is the way.... For he is our model and light."[3] Notice also, that when John of the Cross counsels us near the beginning of his whole major work, his first norm is this: "First, have an habitual desire to imitate Christ in all your deeds by

---

1   A, II, 7, 8.

2   *Ibid.*

3   *Ibid.* 9

bringing your life in conformity with His...in order to...behave in all events as He would."[4]

So, John puts primary emphasis on Jesus as **the way**, as the example we are to imitate. And he often applies this example of Christ to the whole effort of the active and passive nights of the soul, which are his way of describing the spiritual life: "Because...Christ is the way and...this way is a death to our natural selves in the sensory and spiritual parts of the soul...this death is patterned on Christ's. For he is our model and light."[5] Later, in the *Spiritual Canticle*, John of the Cross indicates how this imitation of Christ culminates in being transformed into Christ. He comments on the profound words of St. Paul, "I live, no longer I, but Christ lives in me" (Gal. 2, 20):

> In saying, "[I live no longer I]," he meant that, even though he had life, it was not his, because he was transformed in Christ, and it was divine more than human. He consequently asserts that he does not live, but that Christ lives in him. In accord with this likeness and transformation, we can say that his life and Christ's were one life through union of love.[6]

John notes how Paul's love of Christ transforms him anew, so that his self is lost in Christ, and a symbiosis results between Paul and Christ. John's exegesis of Paul here is very accurate, for Paul refers to a vital union and incorporation into Christ, a mutual belonging; he says that his self is lost in Christ; he speaks, acts, and lives with Christ. Then, he applies these words of Paul to the soul that is being transformed into Christ.

---

4   A, I, 13, 3.

5   A, II, 7, 9; see also *ibid.* 11.

6   SC, XII, 7-8.

When John speaks of Jesus as **the truth,** he surpasses even himself. He teaches us Christians that God "spoke everything to us at once" in his Son; his entire revelation is found in Christ. In the context, John is counseling all his disciples not to seek any revelation other than Jesus himself. For God has no other wisdom or revelation but Jesus:

> In giving us his Son, His only Word...he spoke everything to us at once in this sole Word....[So] God was as it were, mute, with no more to say, because...He has now spoken all at once by giving us the All who is his Son. [To] any person questioning God or desiring some vision or revelation...God could respond as follows: If I have already told you all things in my Word, my Son, and I have no other word, what answer or revelation could I now make that would surpass this? Fasten your eyes on him alone, because in Him...you shall discover even more than you ask for and desire.[7]

Thus, for John there is no other truth or word of God except Jesus our Lord. He is the total truth for us to know and believe. To summarize John of the Cross, then, Jesus is the Way as our model, the Life as the one into whom we are transformed, and the Truth as the whole truth we are to believe.

Now let us consider the Gospel of John itself: "I am the way and the truth and the life. No one comes to the Father except through me" (Jo. 14, 6). The best explanation of this text is found in *The Anchor Bible, Vol. 29A*. Here Fr. Raymond Brown, the premier scholar on John, first discusses various explanations of this text in history; he notes that some scholars emphasize either the way or the truth or the

---

7   A, II, 22, 3-5.

life as primary, so that the other two are subordinate to it, while others scholars consider that all three should have equal emphasis. Then he carefully chooses the explanation "wherein **the way** is the primary predicate and the truth and the life are just explanations of the way. Jesus is the way because he is the truth and the life."[8] His conclusion then is:

> He is the way because he is the truth or revelation of the Father... so that when [people] know him they know the Father (v. 7) and when [they] see him they see the Father (v. 8). He is the way because he is the life – since he lives in the Father and the Father lives in him (vv. 10-11), he is the channel through which the Father's life comes to [all people].[9]

According to this exegesis, when Jesus says "I am the way," he is not **primarily** presenting himself as a moral guide, nor as a leader for his disciples to follow. Rather he is presenting himself as the only **avenue of salvation**. Clearly this primary exegesis of John's Gospel text is different from that of John of the Cross. But Raymond Brown does propose a **secondary meaning** to this text: Jesus is the way as a norm or **model of life**, because John's Gospel thinks of truth not as an abstract system of faith but as a sphere of action. Ray Brown comes to this conclusion only after a lengthy and careful development on "the way of truth". His conclusion is:

> ...John 14, 6 reflects [the] whole chain of usage of the image of "the way" originating in the O. T. [Pss. 86, 11 and 119, 30; Tob.

---

8   Raymond Brown, *The Gospel According to John, XIII-XXI* (NY: Doubleday, 1970), p. 621 (emphasis added).. This is Vol. 29A of *The Anchor Bible)*.

9   *Ibid.* p. 628.

1, 3; Wis. 5, 6], modified by sectarian Jewish thought illustrated at Qumran [The Qumran community designated itself absolutely as "the way".], and finally adopted by the Christian community as a self designation [Acts 9, 2; 19, 9 and 23; 22, 4; 24, 14 and 22].[10]

So this **secondary** meaning of Jesus' words in Scripture is the same as John of the Cross' teaching: Jesus is the Way inasmuch as he is **our model** for believing in him and following in his way.

One of the reasons for this careful comparison between John of the Cross and the Gospel of John here, is that many deny that our saint places sufficient emphasis on the humanity of Christ. Contrary to that opinion, we can summarize John's teaching on the centrality of Christ: 1) we make progress in our Christian life only by imitating Jesus; 2) our whole goal is to bring our life into conformity with his; 3) the means to this goal is to study the life of Christ so that we can behave in all events as he would; 4) Jesus is the whole revelation of the Father; 5) our highest perfection consists in being transformed into Christ so that we live with him. We will continue to see how John's whole outlook is christological; for his model is Christ alone; his truth is nothing but the Word of God, the total revelation of God; and the goal of his life is a transformation into Jesus.

Second, consider what John of the Cross says about the humanity of Jesus in our contemplation. In our contemplation, should we concentrate on the life, passion and death of Jesus? The point of this question is that once we no longer actively meditate with sensible images and intellectual reasonings, there seems to be no room for placing before us the sensible image of the human Jesus in our contemplation.

Let us first look at how Teresa of Avila answers the question about contemplating the humanity of Christ. Her general teaching

---

10   *Ibid.* p. 629.

about contemplation is similar to that of John of the Cross; they both reject sensible images in the practice of contemplation. Yet there is no doubt that Teresa makes a clear exception of the sacred humanity of Jesus. That is, the humanity of Jesus is one image that she still holds onto; she wants us never to lose sight of his life and death even in contemplation:

> ...God desires that if we are going to...receive His great favors, we must do so through the most sacred humanity of Christ.... [W]e must enter by this gate if we desire his sovereign Majesty to show us great secrets. Thus [you]...should desire no other path even if you are at the summit of contemplation. On this road you walk safely.... He will teach us these things. In beholding His life we find that He is the best example.[11]

Thus, even though Teresa of Avila rejects consideration of bodily objects in contemplation, she emphatically adds, "[T]he most sacred humanity of Christ must not be counted in a balance with other corporeal things."[12] And she mentions other saints who followed the same road.

But what does John say about considering the humanity of Jesus? His response is not as explicit as that of Teresa. But he does seem to imply a similar answer. For in his famous passage about Jesus as the total revelation of God to us, he quotes Matthew 17, 5: "This is my beloved Son...listen to him," and several times in the same chapter he paraphrases these words of God:

---

11   Teresa of Avila, *Life* (Washington, DC: ICS Publications, 1976), p. 194 (chapter 22, nos. 6-7). This is part of *The Collected Works of St. Teresa of Avila,* trans. by Kieran Kavanaugh, O.C.D. and Otilio Rodriguez, O.C.D.

12   *Ibid.* p. 195, no. 8.

Fasten your eyes on Him alone, because in him I have spoken and revealed all...;behold Him well, for in him you will uncover all these revelations already made, and many more....Behold my Son, subject to Me and to others out of love for me...; fix your eyes on   him, and you will discern hidden in him the most secret mysteries and wisdom...of God.[13]

That is, we learn all the wisdom of God in contemplating the human Christ, and we find comfort in the suffering Jesus. Admittedly, this passage is found in the *Ascent of Mount Carmel*, which does not treat contemplation specifically. But in the *Spiritual Canticle,* the real human Jesus is the focal point of his whole work, for throughout that entire book, the spouse of the soul is the real human Jesus to whom the soul is betrothed and ultimately married. In general, how can our way and the goal be transformation into the human Jesus, if we do not constantly relate to him as our human lover? As a final conclusion, then, John of the Cross does not exclude the human Jesus as the object of our contemplative prayer.

PARTICULAR VIRTUES OF JESUS OUR MODEL

John of the Cross keeps this general principle of Jesus our model as a frequent motive, especially in the **active dark nights** described in the *Ascent of Mount Carmel.* He applies this principle explicitly regarding certain virtues.

His most frequent application is regarding renunciation of all things that are contrary to the will of God. For example, he quotes Lk. 14, 33: "[E]veryone of you who does not renounce all his possessions cannot be my disciple." Luke's meaning is that Jesus' followers must

---

13   A, II, 22, 5.

not recoil before any sacrifice required of them to see their following of him through to the end, even if this means the sacrifice of all their possessions. John easily translates this call of discipleship into his paradigm:

> [The meaning of Lk. 14, 33] is clear, for the doctrine that the Son of Man came to teach is contempt for all things, that we may receive the gift of God's Spirit. As long as an individual fails to rid himself of these possessions, he is incapable of receiving God's Spirit in pure transformation.[14]

This text, along with Luke 9, 23-24 and the synoptic parallels, contains the whole teaching of John of the Cross on discipleship and on following Jesus our model.

> [This road to God] demands only the one thing necessary: true self-denial, exterior and interior, through surrender of self both to suffering for Christ and to annihilation in all things.... If one fails in this exercise, the root and sum total of all the virtues, the other methods would [fail]....A man makes progress only through imitation of Christ, who is the Way...and this way is death to our natural selves...patterned on Christ's.[15]

We must remember that the above quotes are part of John's paradigm of the active dark night, in which one renounces the desire and affection for all things that are positive obstacles to doing God's will. So the second and allied virtue for John is doing the will of God:

---

14   A, I, 5, 2.

15   A, II, 7, 8-9.

Second, in order to be successful in his imitation [of Christ] renounce and remain empty of any satisfaction that is not purely for the honor and glory of God. Do this out of love for Jesus Christ. In his life he had no other gratification...than the fulfillment of His Father's will, which he called his...food.[16]

In other words, one fair description of John's central teaching of renunciation and dark night is simply seeking to do the will of God in all we do. This may be a very clear and more familiar way for us to understand John. It is also the only universal way to describe what Jesus was about: doing the will of the Father.

Modeling our life on Jesus includes a third virtue, closely connected to the first two, and expressing the highest state of following Jesus; it is the virtue of suffering with Christ crucified.

John presents us with a most human Jesus here, and with the most profound example for us:

...at the moment of his death, [Jesus] was certainly annihilated in His soul...since the Father left that way in innermost aridity.... This was the most extreme abandonment, sensitively, that He had suffered in his life. And by it he accomplished the most marvelous work of His whole life. [Similarly when the spiritual person] is brought to nothing...the spiritual union between his soul and God will be effected. This union is the most noble and sublime state attainable in this life.[17]

Here again John equates the extremes of our following Jesus in the dark night with Jesus' annihilation on the cross. Ruth Burrows has

16 A, I, 13, 4.
17 A, II, 7, 11,

a wonderful commentary of this:

> John of the Cross' doctrine of the night is essentially christological. It makes no sense apart from Christ crucified who is the wisdom and power of God.... John points us to Jesus in the great act of redemption, stripped of all, emptied out, brought to nothing. If we are to receive all God wants to give us, brought to nothing. If we are to receive all God wants to give us, we too must enter into this mystery of self-emptying.[18]

What both these writers are telling us is that Jesus himself, especially on the cross, is the paradigm of the highest perfection. That is, Jesus on the cross dramatized in an objective, historical, visible way what takes place interiorly, implicitly and secretly in the authentic mystical life.

All of this is close to Jesus' call in Luke's Gospel, "If anyone wishes to come after me, he must deny himself and take up his cross daily and follow me" (Lk. 9, 23). For the likely meaning of "take up his cross daily" is to have the courage to live each day for Christ and his cause, so that Jesus' radical challenge includes our following in his footsteps and living "the way" each day.

Finally modeling our life on Jesus includes the virtue of love of our neighbor. Admittedly, we find few references to this virtue in John's description of Jesus as our model. His reasoning seems to be that our love of God necessarily includes love of our neighbor as in Mk. 12, 29-31. Probably John's best commentary on Jesus here, is found in his "Spiritual Sayings" (described by Fray Eliseo):

---

18   Ruth Burrows, *Ascent to Love,* p.96.

...love for...one's neighbor is born of the spiritual and contemplative life...[by which] we are clearly commanded...to have this zeal for the profit of our neighbor...for [religious] include within themselves two lives, the active and the contemplative, in one. This mixed life the Lord chose for himself because it is the most perfect....And it is clearly true that compassion for our neighbor grows the more, according as the soul is more closely united with God through love; the more we love, the more we desire that this same God shall be loved...by all. And the more we desire this, the more we labor for it, both in prayer and in all other...exercises.[19]

Surprisingly, nowhere does John of the Cross quote that one commandment of John's Gospel: "[L]ove one another as I love you" (Jo. 15, 12). But let us consider it now. What Jesus offers here is his own supreme act of love in laying down his life for others as the model for our love. In the parallel passage (Jo. 13, 34), Jesus calls this his **new** commandment. It is a new commandment because it has an entirely new model, Jesus himself, and because it is the basic stipulation of the New Covenant. This new covenant was intimated in Jeremiah: "I will make a new covenant with the house of Israel.... I will place my law within them, and write it upon their hearts...." (Jer. 31, 31-33). This intimate knowledge is equivalent to love and is a covenantal virtue. So Jesus' new commandment of love is central to his new covenant (Lk, 22, 20) and is all-inclusive of our whole following of Jesus. Now John of the Cross tells us constantly that the

---

19 Fray Eliseo de los Martires, "Spiritual Sayings Attributed to St. John of the Cross," Sixth Saying. This is found in *The Complete Works of St. John of the Cross, Vol III,* trans. E. Allison Peers (Westminster, MD: The Newman Press, 1953), p. 291-292. Notice that these sayings are only "attributed to St. John of the Cross."

goal of contemplative prayer is our complete union with God in love. And he is aware that love of God includes love of our neighbor: "... as the love of neighbor increases, the love of God increases and vice versa."[20] But he never makes the explicit connection between Jesus' words, "Love one another as I love you," and his own constant teaching about our love of God.

SUGGESTION FOR PRAYER

One example of prayer flows naturally from what we have just considered.

Lord Jesus you alone are the Way, the Truth and the Life. As the **Way** you are the only model for me to imitate. You are the example and light of my life; I want to conform my life to yours, to follow in your footsteps, to behave as you behaved. To live as you lived is the sum of holiness. I know, Lord, this has nothing to do with my state in life: married or single, religious or lay, daily work or secular achievement. It has everything to do with your teaching, your life, and your person as the way of human wholeness. You are the complete model for me by exemplifying norms and values for human living, by inviting me to new attitudes, by giving a new meaning to life, by drawing me to new dispositions, by motivating me with love, be encouraging me with hope.

Loving Jesus, you are the **Life** for me to live, so that with Paul I might say, "I live, no longer I, but Christ lives in me." As you were united with the Father even in your humanity, so you invite me to be transformed into you; as your words and wisdom were only your Father's, so you want me to know and express your words; as your works and power were all dependent on your Father, so any spiritual power I have is yours; without you, I can do nothing. As you came

---

20   A, III, 23, 1.

only "to do the will of [your] Father," so I want only "your kingdom come, your will be done." As you abided in your Father's love, so you want me to "remain in [your] love." As you were totally united with the Father, so you want me to be transformed into you in love. Without you Lord, I am nothing. When I surrender to you and depend on your life of grace, I fulfill my whole life.

You, gentle Jesus, are the **Truth**. God himself has no other wisdom or revelation to give us than you, who are his Word. I look for no other answers, no other expression of God, no other understanding of human life, no other truth to believe. To see you is to see God, to know you is to know God, to believe in you is to gain eternal life.

In sum Lord, you are the Way as my model for living, the Life as the one into whom I can be transformed, the Truth as the whole truth about God and revelation that I am to believe.

Chapter 6
The Secret to Contemplation

In the previous chapters, we considered a number of issues that are necessary for us to understand the practice of contemplation. In this chapter, let us begin to study John of the Cross' teaching about contemplation, along with his secret of contemplation.

When John begins his treatment of the *Dark Night, Book I,* he entitles it "a treatise on the passive night of the senses;" and adds, "this dark night signifies...purgative contemplation."[1] What he means by **dark night** is that the memory, understanding and will are dark and empty. That is, just as actual night leaves the eyes dark and unable to function, so dark contemplation leaves our memory, intellect and will dark and unable to function. And he calls this the **passive** dark night of the senses because "at this time God does not communicate himself through the senses as he did before...but begins to communicate himself through pure spirit by an act of simple contemplation, in which there is no discursive succession of thoughts."[2] That is, because our intellect can only function naturally by means of sense knowledge, it is incapable of experiencing the immediate presence of God. So only if we shut down this natural way of knowing can we open ourselves to the immediate infusion of divine knowledge. That is why the dark night is necessary at the beginning of contemplation and why darkness and emptiness is the secret to contemplation for John of the Cross.

Let us recall again our common experience of prayer. After years of practicing meditation of various kinds, our prayer naturally becomes more simple. Not only are we without engaging ideas to occupy us or

---

1   DN, I, prologue, 1
2   *Ibid.* 9, 8.

spontaneous affections to hearten us, there is not even a sense of sitting at the feet of Jesus in simple love. There is no clarity of thought, distinctness of image, nor sensible fervor. We eventually become frustrated and confused because we seem to be getting nowhere; we begin to feel that our prayer life has reached a dead end. We didn't realize, then, is that our prayer life was developing naturally. That is, our experience was following a natural progression from discursive mental prayer to more affective prayer to simpler prayer and then to quiet, passive prayer.

Such dark and unsatisfying prayer was not a dead end. John wants us to know that this stage of prayer is quite necessary; without it, we could not go further. In John's own words: "[God] desires to withdraw them from [meditation]...and lead them on to a higher degree of divine love...in which they become capable of a communion with God that is more abundant...."[3] His point is that this dark night brings our intellect into obscurity and closes the door to our former way of meditation so that God may grant a new, divine light to the soul:

> [T]his dark contemplation must first purge and annihilate it of its natural light and bring it actually into obscurity. It is fitting that this darkness last as long as is necessary for the expulsion and annihilation of the intellect's natural way of understanding...and that the divine light and illumination take its place.[4]

Again and again, John cautions those who are beginning to practice contemplation that they must cease all sensible images, rational thoughts and discursive reasoning and "learn to be empty of all things...and live in pure nakedness and poverty of spirit."[5] He wants us

---

3   *Ibid.* 8, 3.

4   DN, II, 9, 3.

5   A, II, 15, 5.

to be "poor in spirit" by ceasing all our natural activities of meditation which obstruct God's supernatural infusion of contemplation. For only when we cease all our natural activities of meditation can we be simply open, attentive and receptive to God. That is, as we progress in contemplation, the senses and intellect become more and more empty, dark and void – that is, spiritually poor – so that God can freely work in the soul.

Why must all those natural activities cease in order for contemplation to replace them? The reason is that contemplation is a new and transcendent way of experiencing God that is contrary to the natural way of knowing and "two contraries cannot coexist in one subject" at the same time.[6]

This is **the key** to understanding John of the Cross' teaching about contemplation. He uses several terms to describe this necessary condition for beginning contemplation. The general term he uses is "dark night."[7] Sometimes, he refers to "poverty of spirit:" "[T]he soul must first be set in emptiness and poverty of spirit and purged of every natural support, consolation and apprehension.... Thus empty, it is truly poor in spirit...and thereby [ready] for the state of union with God...."[8] Frequently, John refers to "emptiness:" "[I]t is fitting that [the soul] be brought into emptiness and poverty...and left in dryness and darkness."[9] But he considers these and similar terms to be almost the same: "emptiness, darkness and nakedness regarding all things or... spiritual poverty (...are all the same)."[10] When taken together, then, all these terms are the key to John of the Cross' teaching on contemplation.

---

6   DN, II, 9, 2.

7   See: DN, I, 8, 3; 9, 7; DN, II, 5, 3; 9, 2-3; 15, 1; 16, 4; 16, 7.

8   DN, II, 9, 4. See also: A, II, 15, 4; DN, II, 4, 1; 6, 4-5.

9   *Ibid.* 6, 4. See also: A, II, 15, 5;A, III, 2, 2; DN, I, 9, 4; 12, 1; DN, II, 8, 4; 16, 1; LF, III, 18 and 46.

10   A, II, 24, 8. Also: DN, II, 4, 1.

All of this helps to explain the great contribution that John of the Cross made to our spiritual theology; that is, the Dark Night is an integral part of the development of prayer.

But we can be even more specific. For John, the Dark Night is the dominant idea, the *leit motif* for his whole teaching on the beginning of contemplation. He insists that darkness, emptiness and poverty of our natural faculties is a necessary condition for contemplation:

> [T]hese faculties must...be darkened...so that... annihilated in their natural way they might lose that lowly and human mode of...working...[and] be prepared for the sublime reception, experience, and savor of the divine and supernatural, which is unreceivable until the old man dies."[11]

Similarly, John teaches that being empty and unhindered by natural reasoning is a requirement for God's infused knowledge: "God also, by means of this dark...contemplation, supernaturally instructs... the soul that is empty and unhindered (which is the requirement for his divine inflow)...."[12] He wants us to know that this dark night has a singular purpose:

> [E]ven though this happy night darkens the spirit, it does so only to impart light concerning all things;...and even though it impoverishes and empties him of all...natural affection, it does so only that he may reach out divinely to the enjoyment of all earthly and heavenly things....[13]

Finally, John of the Cross assures us that once we are empty of

---

11 DN, II, 16, 4. Also: *Ibid.* 9, 4.
12 See DN, I, 12, 4.
13 DN, II, 9, 1.

all sense images and reasoning of ordinary meditation, God will do his part: "When the soul frees itself of all things and attains to emptiness and dispossession concerning them...it is impossible that God fail to do his part by communicating Himself to it, at least secretly and silently."[14]

He even offers this assurance: "As soon as natural things are driven out of the enamored soul, the divine are naturally and supernaturally infused, since there can be no void in nature."[15] This image is particularly forceful in our day, because we are so familiar with vacuum-packed coffee cans. As soon as we puncture the lid, the outside atmosphere fills the void with a hiss of air rushing in. In a similar way, once our prayer becomes empty of all sensible images and intellectual thought, then the divine peace and calm of God's presence will be supernaturally infused to fill the emptiness, for "there can be no void in nature." For John of the Cross then, this is the secret, the key to contemplation: once our prayer becomes empty of all sensible images and intellectual thought, God will communicate himself directly to us at least secretly and silently.

Let me add a note here about the approach I will use throughout this book. It will follow the method of John of the Cross in describing the secret of contemplation. His method is to **repeat this secret many times**, and sometimes to approach that theme from different angles or with different emphases. Apparently, he is convinced that this kind of repetition is almost necessary in order to make this essential point about the beginning of contemplation, because such a practice of darkness and emptiness is so foreign to our natural way of meditation. In this book then, I will **often repeat** his same secret about contemplation, as

---

14   LF, III, 46. Ftn. 7 on p. 23 explains that this quote is about the beginning of contemplation.

15   A, II, 15, 4 .

well as his other critical teachings about how to act in contemplation, and also his words of encouragement to be confident in this dark night. I myself had to read and pray over some of his oft-repeated counsels, again and again, until they finally sank in. So I ask your indulgence when you read such repetitions over and over in several of the remaining chapters. Hopefully, repeating the same critical ideas and coming at them from different angles or with different emphases will deeply impress on us the need to practice this form of prayer that seems so foreign to us.

JOHN'S THREE SIGNS OF CONTEMPLATION

Let me first note that in his *Ascent of Mount Carmel, Book II*, John offers three signs by which we know that we are in the **active night of the spirit**. [16] These are his signs to guide us when meditation is becoming more dark and simple, so that we can begin to discontinue meditation: "[These three signs indicate] when one ought to discontinue meditation…so that the practice will not be abandoned sooner or later than that required by the spirit."[17] His whole treatment there deals with the latter stages of **active meditation.**

But when John begins to treat the **passive night of sense**, in the *Dark Night, Book I*, he offers three signs as a practical help for us to know that we should practice **contemplation** regularly in our prayer.[18] Even though the two sets of signs seem similar, they relate to different situations. We want to concentrate here on the three signs marking the **passive night of sense.** They focus exactly on our topic here, which is the transition from meditation to the beginning of contemplation.

---

16   A, II, 13, 2-4.

17   A, II, 13, 1.

18   DN, I, 9 (whole chapter).

The first [sign] is that as these souls do not get satisfaction or consolation from the things of God, they do not get any out of creatures either... He does not allow [them] to find sweetness or delight in anything.[19]

He means that no sensible pleasures really satisfy us as before; we find satisfaction in nothing, and we no longer get consolation from our prayer. Notice that John is speaking here not only about our interior prayer but our whole external life as well.

The second sign...is that the memory ordinarily turns to God solicitously and with painful care, and the soul thinks it is not serving God, but turning back, because it is aware of this distaste for the things of God.[20]

That is, our care is generally centered on God; we are conscious of the need to serve him, along with anxiety not to fail him. What we did with alacrity before, we now find difficult in our state of aridity and emptiness.

The third sign...is the powerlessness...to meditate and make use of the Imagination...as was one's previous custom. At this time God...begins to communicate himself by an act of simple contemplation... As a result the imaginative powers and fantasy can no longer rest in any consideration nor find support in it.[21]

Here the difficulty to meditate grows even greater; soon there

---

19   *Ibid.* 9, 2.

20   *Ibid.* 3.

21   *Ibid.* 8

is a constant inability, more absolute than the preparatory stage of simple prayer. The old forms of meditation are no longer useful, while the new form of contemplation comes so gradually and is so tenuous and confusing to us. Our prayer often feels empty to us; our personal activity has been reduced to nothing. Yet at the same time, this new perception of God is only an undefined intimation of his presence. At worst it is nothing but a void; at best it is so tenuous and slight that we doubt its reality. For a time, there is no more than a gleam in the night that doesn't seem to become nearer or clearer. Only slowly do we give up our self-sufficiency and learn to be open and receptive to God's subtle action.

SUGGESTION FOR PRAYER

In John's Gospel, the five Paraclete sayings of Jesus can help guide us into infused contemplation. (That is: 14, 16-17; 14, 25-26; 15, 26-27; 16, 8-11; 16, 12-13.) For the main thrust of Jesus' promise of the Paraclete is that the Spirit will teach us everything we need to know about Jesus and God; the Spirit will abide with us and guide us to all truth. Certainly that does not exclude the infused wisdom of the spirit of Truth, which is the most sublime and complete knowledge we can ever learn. Infused knowledge can only come to us by means of the spirit of Truth within us. All of these works of the Paraclete are active and effective during our prayer, especially during contemplative prayer. Every time we begin our contemplative prayer we can begin by remembering these wonderful promises of Jesus and praying with great assurance.

These promises of Jesus will also help us when we encounter darkness, weakness or aridity in our contemplation. The very nature of contemplative prayer drives us to rely on the Holy Spirit, for the essential nature of this prayer is passive and dependent on the infused wisdom of the Spirit. As John of the Cross describes this prayer at the beginning of contemplation:

> This communication [through contemplation] is secret and dark to the work of the intellect and the other faculties. Insofar as these faculties do not acquire it but the Holy Spirit infuses it and puts it in order in the soul,...the soul neither knows nor understands how this comes to pass and thus calls it secret.[22]

---

22   DN, II, 17, 2.

Chapter 7
The Dark Night, In Other Words

John of the Cross describes the beginning of contemplation as a dark night. It is a **night** because all the natural faculties of the soul – the memory, the intellect and the will – are dark and empty. It is **infused contemplation**, because it is the direct inflow of God in the soul. His terminology – of the dark night of the senses and of the spirit – is his trademark. It is quite distinct from the terminology of other contemplative writers. However, what these classical writers say about the practice and experience of contemplation is not substantially different from that of John of the Cross. Their descriptions of the beginning of contemplation basically agree with John's, though they use their own terminology. We might say that they teach John's dark night in other words.

There are five characteristics that John and the classical writers agree on. 1. The transition from meditation to infused contemplation is usually **gradual and quite natural.** That is, it is quite natural for our meditation to grow more and more simple. There is no clarity of thought, distinctness of image, nor sensible fervor. We feel that we are getting nowhere; our prayer life seems to fade away and become empty. 2. The beginning of contemplation is usually affected in a **scarcely perceptible way.** There may be brief, dark touches or subtle and tenuous experiences. But generally, the experience does not include clear images or distinct notions. 3. In contemplation, we actually experience that God is present within us; that experience is derived not only from the assurance of faith but also from a **direct, immediate contact** with the divine goodness. 4. We receive this experience **passively**, not as a result of our own efforts; it is infused by the direct action of God. We cannot obtain it, retain it or regain it by ourselves. Yet we know that we are acted upon and caught up in God. 5. **Only this sense of God's presence and action is essential** to infused contemplation. All other phenomena (such as rapture, ecstasy, distinct vision, interior locution) are not necessary elements of contemplation. Modern authors are also insistent that these phenomena are separable from contemplation; they need not be present at all.

In this chapter, we want to compare what other classical writers say about these five characteristics. They do not use John's terminology of the dark night. Studying their descriptions of contemplation, can add to our understanding of these characteristics and give us new insights into John's terminology.

1. NATURAL TRANSITION

Both Teresa of Avila and John of the Cross treat the transition from discursive meditation to the beginning of contemplation as a **natural development** of prayer. That is, they explain that discursive meditation tends to become more simple and dark, and that such prayer is not the end of the line but the preparation for beginning contemplation. That is why they are very careful to offer norms for leaving meditation and turning to contemplation.

When we consider these norms, we understand how they see this transition as quite natural. When spiritual writers compare Teresa of Avila and John of the Cross on their norms for transitioning from meditation to contemplation, they are not inclined to show how similar they are. Much of their hesitation stems from the fact that John has two sets of signs: 1) In the *Ascent of Mount Carmel*, John has three signs "for recognizing... when [one] should discontinue discursive meditation."[1] These are part of the **active** dark night or the transition

---

1   A, II, all of chapter 13.

from meditation to contemplation. Then in the *Dark Night*, John has three signs marking the **passive** dark night or the beginning of contemplation.[2] It is not surprising that some confuse these two sets of signs, for they sound superficially similar. But only the three signs in the *Ascent of Mount Carmel* actually deal with the transition from meditation to contemplation.

And when these signs are compared to those of Teresa of Avila, they are quite similar. Notice how Teresa counsels those who are in transition from meditation to contemplation:

> [I]f his Majesty has not begun to inebriate us [in the prayer of recollection – {her first stage of contemplative prayer}], I do not see how the mind can be prevented from discoursing, without doing more harm than good....It is to be understood...that meditation must cease only when love is awakened in the soul.... What I believe is most meet for the soul...is...that without the least force...it should endeavor to cease to discourse with the understanding, but not to suspend its activity entirely.[3]

This teaching of Teresa of Avila is very similar to John's first sign for discontinuing meditation:

> As long as one can...make discursive meditation and draw out satisfaction, one must not abandon this method. Meditation must only be discontinued when the soul is placed in that peace and quietude [of beginning contemplation].[4]

---

2   DN, I, all of chapter 9. Notice that in 9, 7 John clearly refers these signs to "this state of contemplation."

3   Teresa of Avila, *The Interior Castle* (Westminster, MD: The Newman Press, 1945), pp. 37-39.

4   A, II, 13, 2.

Apparently then, both John and Teresa teach that as long as we can continue with meditation, we should not force ourselves to depart from the natural stage we are in or abandon it, unless God begins to draw us on to the new way of prayer.

Once we recognize that both of these great mystical writers teach the same thing about the transition from meditation to contemplation, we can have greater confidence in following their common counsel.

2. SCARCELY PERCEPTIBLE

Classical writers agree with John of the Cross that the beginning of contemplation is usually a **subtle and tenuous experience**. Compare his teaching with that of Yves Raguin:

> When prayer has become very simple…there appears in the soul a new element, a new imperceptible presence, which is so tenuous, so slight, so circumspect, so close to absence, that it is almost impossible to distinguish it from that mysterious perception which accompanies the knowledge derived from faith. [F]or a long time it can only be a gleam in the night….[5]

How similar Yves Raguin's explanation here is to John's continuous description of the dark night at the beginning of contemplation.

Another classic writer on prayer, A. Poulain, teaches that this obscurity is one of the essential characteristics of contemplation (which he refers to as "mystic union'):

---

5   Yves Raguin, S.J., *Paths to Contemplation* (Wheathamstead, England: Anthony Clarke, 1987), p. 116.

[Another] character of the mystic union consists in the fact that the knowledge of God…is obscure and confused…. Beginners… never suspect that it always remains indistinct…. Hence their astonishment when the prayer of quiet is first granted to them; they see it as a preliminary state only, out of which some distinct knowledge will soon make its way.[6]

This characteristic is mentioned again and again by spiritual writers. They agree that the presence of God is scarcely perceptible, especially in the beginning of contemplation.

3. EXPERIENCE OF GOD'S PRESENCE

Thomas Merton is one of the leading teachers of contemplation in the twentieth century. Notice how he describes the **experience of God's presence** at the beginning of contemplation:

The most important thing of all is to get some realization of what God is doing in your soul…. [This dark night brings] you to the threshold of an actual experimental contact with the living God. In fact, John of the Cross does not hesitate to say that this darkness is caused by the presence of God in the intellect…. [God] is now beginning to infuse into the soul His own Light and His own Love in one general confused experience….[7]

---

6   A. Poulain, S. J., *The Graces of Interior Prayer* (London: Routledge and Kegan Paul Lim. 1951), p. 118.

7   Thomas Merton, *The Inner Experiencer* (San Francisco: HarperCollins Publishers, 2003), pp. 95-96. William Shannon edited this work after Merton's death. Notice that Merton uses the word, "experimental," here. Would the word, "experiencial," be more appropriate?

Throughout this book, *The Inner Experiences,* Merton continues to describe "this dark and loving knowledge of God" as the essence of contemplation.

Later in this chapter, we will note other characteristics of his spiritual teaching on contemplation that parallels that of John.

Mathieu Rousset, O.P. even calls this sense of God's presence "the foundation, the *raison d'etre*" of contemplation: The experimental knowledge of God's...presence within us is the foundation, the *raison d'etre* of...the mystic life."[8] A. Poulain calls this experience of God's presence "the first fundamental character" of contemplation:

> The real point of difference from the recollection of ordinary prayer is this...[God] gives us an experimental...knowledge of his presence.... In the...prayer of quiet, God only does this in a somewhat obscure manner. The manifestation increases in distinctness as the union becomes of a higher order.[9]

4. PASSIVE EXPERIENCE

Perhaps the most famous quote in all of patristic writing about contemplation is that of Denis the Areopagite (Pseudo-Dionysius):

> As far as possible, raise thyself up in unknowing even unto union with Him Who is beyond...all knowledge...to the pure and superessential ray of the divine darkness.... [T]hus united in the most noble union with Him who is utterly unknowable, by

---

8   Mathieu Rousset, O.P., *La Doctrine Spirituelle, Vol VII,* Book I, Ch. 15. This quote is also found in A. Poulain, *The Graces of Interior Prayer* (ftn. 6 above), p. 82.

9   A. Poulain, *opus cit.,* pp. 64-65.

the cessation of all knowledge; in this total unknowing he now knows with a knowledge that is beyond understanding.[10]

This "ray of darkness" is quoted again and again by modern writers on contemplation. They do not agree on its precise meaning, but my sense of it is that contemplation offers an experience of God that is often without any accompanying intellectual light or understanding. That is, though the intellect understands nothing, there is an experience of the presence of God; the "ray" is a sense of God's presence; the "darkness" refers to the lack of intellectual light.

When Thomas Merton comments on this very passage, he stresses that this experience is **entirely passive**:

> In the darkness of unknowing, the contemplative passively receives the touch of divine knowledge…. Traditionally, the most characteristic note of Christian contemplation is this passivity, this reception of divine light-in-darkness as a supremely mysterious and unaccountable gift of God's love.[11]

5. ONLY GOD'S PRESENCE IS ESSENTIAL

Throughout John of the Cross' teaching about the beginning of contemplation, he wants us to know that the essence of this prayer is the experience of God's presence: "[C]ontemplation is nothing else than a secret and peaceful and loving inflow of God…."[12] He teaches that the normal way of contemplation in the beginning is without emotional states or clear vision – nor are they essential; the **only all-inclusive sign** of contemplation is absorption in God. Even in the most advanced

---

10 See: Thomas Merton, *The Inner Experience,* pp. 71-72.

11 *Ibid.,* p. 72.

12 DN, I, 10, 6.

forms of contemplation, the unitive way, there is no requirement of other phenomena: "This spiritual marriage…is a total transformation in the Beloved in which…[there is] a total consummation of the union of love."[13]

Yves Raguin clarifies, more than most, what is the essence of contemplation:

> The development of contemplation…[starts] when the divine presence begins to show itself.… [T]here appears in the soul…a new perceptible presence, which is so tenuous, so slight.… Soon this presence becomes clear.… [It] seems to surge up from the depths of the soul's being.… If the soul is faithful in its attention, this presence will increase.… [God] sends an immense peace into the soul, consoling it, strengthening it, enriching it with virtues, enlightening it and revealing His love to it.[14]

Here Raguin notes that "Soon this presence becomes clear" and "this presence will increase." So, he connects the advance in contemplative prayer with a greater sense of God's presence, without mentioning any other phenomena.

However, the point of this fifth characteristic goes beyond this somewhat; it claims that in all the stages of contemplative prayer the **one essential experience** is that of the presence of God, which in the higher stages includes a more intimate union and an all-engrossing love of God. All the other phenomena (rapture, ecstasy, visions, locutions) are certainly amazing graces of union with God, but those precise phenomena are not required for contemplation.

---

13   SC, 22, 3.

14   Ives Raguin, *Paths to Contemplation,* pp. 116-117.

The classical spiritual writer, Jean Gerson, describes all the stages of contemplation in an all-inclusive definition: "[A]n exact, condensed definition of mystic theology [is]: "It is an experimental perception of God."[15] He adds that the unique object of mystic prayer is ""an experimental knowledge of God in the embrace of unitive love."[16] Thus, Gerson also makes no mention of other phenomena as essential to the stages of contemplation.

It is true that both classical writers and modern writers mention several other characteristics of contemplation besides these five. They certainly do not agree on all the characteristics, nor even the number of them. But these are five characteristics of contemplation that they do agree on. They do not use John of the Cross' terminology of the dark nights, but they describe these same stages of contemplation using their own terminology. We might say they teach John's dark nights in other words.

SUGGESTION FOR PRAYER

One suggestion for our beginning of daily prayer is to reflect on one of these five commonly agreed characteristics of prayer. Just reviewing one of these counsels from classical writers can set our mind in the proper attitude for prayer.

Besides these five characteristics of prayer, there are some very basic suggestions that various spiritual writers teach about the time of prayer. One general practical suggestion for all our daily prayer is to set aside a definite time for prayer each day. The period should be somewhat regular and last for twenty to twenty-five minutes. The time

---

15   Jean Gerson, *On the Magnificat* (Antwerp, 1706), tr. 7, ch. 2. This is quoted by Poulain, *opus cit.,* p. 81.

16   Jean Gerson, *Theologia Mystica,* no. 28. This is quoted by Poulain, *opus cit.,* p. 110.

of the day we choose should be free of external distractions, such as phone calls and other electronic communications. They also add that we cannot progress unless we pray regularly.

Another practical suggestion may help us overcome our reluctance to pray when our prayer seems very dark over a long period of time. We may have to make some accommodations to human nature. That is, our prayer may be so dark and difficult that we may need some respite in the way we pray. In my case, I could no longer pray at a *prie-dieu* or in a quiet corner. In addition, for a time I was burned out by the demands of my ministry. My spiritual director told me about an abbot he knew who contemplated while walking outdoors. I also knew that John of the Cross himself used to recite his morning office outdoors before mass. I knew there were some nice parks nearby that were not busy during the day, so I found time each day to go there and sit on a park bench to contemplate in a quiet and bright setting. Some other alternatives are recommended by others, such as quiet music, incense or a lighted candle; they tend to help center the mind and heart in prayer. Such temporary changes can help us through this transition, when we can no longer pray in the way we were accustomed. Such external accommodations can offer some pleasant surroundings when our prayer is oppressive. Internally, however, we still approach God as always – by being open and attentive to God's Spirit.

Chapter 8
Images of Contemplation

Those who were not very familiar with the writings of John of the Cross might be surprised to discover his constant use of poetry, as well as countless images and metaphors, in order to describe the experience of contemplation. He is quite convinced that the experience is ineffable and indescribable. So, he constantly uses poetry to offer various images that help our prayer. Thus, a single poem of eight verses forms the basis for the three books of *Ascent of Mount Carmel* as well as the two books of the *Dark Night*. Also the entire book of the *Spiritual Canticle* is a line-by-line exposition and commentary on a poem or canticle of forty verses.

Each of these poems is filled with metaphors and images that John of the Cross constantly refers to in his description of contemplative prayer. These poetic images stir up our imagination and engage our intellect in ways that are so much more effective than abstract ideas. Some of his metaphors are quite famous, such as the "dark nights of sense and spirit," and "the bride and bridegroom." But his poetic images include an endless array of nature scenes: woods and thickets, hills and meadows, valleys and rock caverns, vineyards and flowers, foxes and lions, wounded stag and white dove, wine and fruit. For example, see *The Spiritual Canticle* stanzas 13 to 21 for the illuminative way and 22 to 35 for the unitive way; these stanzas are filled with such poetic images. In a word, the ineffable experience of contemplation is given some measure of clarity and appeal by means of countless engaging images.

Following the method of John of the Cross, then, this article will suggest various metaphors and images that will help those who are beginning contemplation to have "a loving and peaceful attentiveness

65

to God." We recall that this is the one necessary attitude:

> The attitude necessary in the night of sense [at the beginning of contemplation] is to pay no attention to discursive meditation, since this is not the time for it. [The soul] should remain in rest and quietude, even though it may seem obvious to them that they are doing nothing and wasting time.... They must be content simply with a **loving and peaceful attentiveness** to God and live without concern, without the effort and without the desire to taste and feel Him.[1]

So, when we can no longer meditate with sensible images, imaginations, rational thoughts and affections, we should not continue to struggle with our natural faculties but "remain in rest and quietude" with "a loving and peaceful attentiveness to God." That is, we should be content to be passive in our prayer; our only activity can be summed up in one word: attentive. Only when we put to rest all our sensible ways of knowing, will there be room for this direct, infused experience of God. Our entire effort is to remain quiet, peaceful, open and receptive to this new experience of God's presence. "Thus the individual also should proceed only with a loving attention to God, without making specific acts. He should conduct himself passively...without efforts of his own, but with simple, loving awareness."[2]

The images that follow are generally those of John of the Cross and are particularly appropriate for those who are beginning to contemplate. We will not make use of those images that John relates to advanced contemplation, only those he chooses in order to describe early contemplation.

---

1   DN. I, 10, 4 (emphasis added).
2   LF, III, 33.

A. DARK NIGHT

The most famous metaphor that John of the Cross uses is that of dark night. The *Dark Night, Book I*, is entitled "a treatise on the passive night of the senses." John says "this dark night signifies...purgative contemplation."[3] He means that the memory, understanding and will are dark and empty. That is, just as actual night leaves the eyes dark and unable to function, so dark contemplation leaves our memory, understanding and will dark and unable to function. And he calls this the passive dark night of the senses because "at this time God does not communicate himself through the senses as he did before...but begins to communicate himself through pure spirit by an act of simple contemplation, in which there is no discursive succession of thoughts."[4]

John is very encouraging for those experiencing this dark night of the senses. He wants us to know that this very inability to meditate is the necessary condition for the beginning of contemplation:

> At the time of the aridities of this sensory night, God [withdraws] the soul from the life of the sense and [places] it in that of the spirit - that is, he brings it from meditation to contemplation - where the soul no longer has the power to...meditate with its faculties on the things of God.[5]

That is, because our intellect can only function naturally by means of sense knowledge, it is incapable of experiencing the immediate presence of God. So only if we shut down this natural way of knowing can we open ourselves to the immediate infusion of divine knowledge. That is why the dark night is necessary at the beginning of

---

3 DN, I, prologue, 1.

4 *Ibid.* 9, 8.

5 *Ibid.* 10, 1.

contemplation and why darkness and emptiness is the hallmark of the beginning of contemplation for John of the Cross.

B. CLOSING THE DOOR

Once more, let us recall the common experience of prayer. After years of practicing meditation, our prayer becomes more simple. Not only are we without engaging ideas to occupy us or spontaneous affections to hearten us, there is not even a sense of sitting at the feet of Jesus in simple love. There is no clarity of thought, distinctness of image not sensible fervor. We become frustrated and confused because we seem to be getting nowhere; our prayer life seems to fade away; we begin to feel that our interior life has reached a closed door, a dead end. What we didn't realize then is that our prayer life was developing naturally and positively. That is, our experience was following a natural progression from discursive mental prayer to more affective prayer, to simpler prayer and then to quiet, passive prayer.

Such dark and unsatisfying prayer was not a closed door; we were not up against a wall. John wants us to know that this stage of prayer is quite necessary; without it, we could not go farther. This is actually the great contribution of John of the Cross to Christian spirituality:

"Perhaps the greatest debt that Christianity owes to John of the Cross is for the clarity with which he showed that the Dark Night of the Soul was not a dead loss in the spiritual life...but was an **integral part** of the development of prayer."[6] In John's own words: "[God] desires to withdraw them from [meditation]...and lead them on to a higher degree of divine love...in which they become capable of a communion with God that is more abundant...."[7] He "closes the door...[and] now leaves

---

6   Leonard Boase, S. J., *The Power of Faith* (Chicago: Loyola Press, 1985), p. 78 (emphasis added).

7   DN, I, 8, 3.

them in such darkness that they do not know which way to turn...now that the interior sensory faculties are engulfed in this night."[8]

That is, this dark night brings our intellect into obscurity and closes the door to our former way of meditation that God may freely grant a new, divine light:

> [T]his dark contemplation must first purge and annihilate it of its natural light and bring it actually into obscurity. It is fitting that this darkness last as long as is necessary for the expulsion and annihilation of the intellect's natural way of understanding...and that the divine light and illumination take its place.[9]

C. AS BABES IN ARMS

One image John gives for the beginning of contemplation is that of a small child being carried. But he offers it in a resistant form:

> Some souls...hamper [God] by their indiscreet activity or resistance. They resemble children who kick and cry and struggle to walk by themselves when their mothers want to carry them; in walking by themselves they make no headway....[10]

John wants us not to resist but to remain peaceful and quiet in the hands of God - content to be helpless and powerless:

> [A] person should not mind if the operations of his faculties are being lost to him; he ought to desire rather that this be done quickly so that he may be no obstacle to the operation

---

8   *Ibid.*

9   DN, II, 9, 3.

10   A, I, prologue, 3.

of the infused contemplation which God is bestowing....For contemplation is nothing else than a secret and peaceful and loving inflow of God.[11]

Time and again John mentions this powerlessness to meditate at the beginning of contemplation: "[God brings the soul] from meditation to contemplation – where the soul no longer has the power to work or meditate with its faculties on the things of God...."[12] Because this powerlessness is the very way forward to a new form of prayer, John wants us simply to let ourselves be carried in the arms of God.

Let me offer various images to describe this helplessness of babes in arms. Perhaps one or more will be of help in our prayer. 1. There is nothing we can do to water this garden; even when we bring up buckets from the well of meditation, they have no nurturing water in them. Only God can send the water of infused contemplation. 2. All our efforts cannot open this door to the direct experience of God; the most we can do is remove all the obstacles on our side. 3. We find ourselves in a rarified air; we need a new way of breathing. Only the pure oxygen of the Spirit of God will sustain us at this altitude. 4. We are way beyond our depth here in this body of water; all we can do is float and wait for God to carry us along.

D. EMPTY VESSEL

Another image John offers for one at the beginning of contemplation is that of the empty vessel: "...until it possesses the loved object and is satisfied...the soul is like an empty vessel waiting to be filled...or like one suspended in air with nothing to lean on."[13]

---

11   DN, I, 10, 6.

12   See DN, I, 10, 1; *ibid.* 9, 8.

13   SC, IX, 6.

Such emptiness in the dark night is a necessary preparation for contemplation:

> ...the soul must first be set in emptiness and poverty of spirit and purged of every support, consolation and apprehension.... Thus empty, it is...thereby able to live that new and blessed life which is the state of union with God, attained by means of this night.[14]

This image of the empty vessel leads John to one of his most encouraging assurances that God will do his part: "When the soul frees itself of all things and attains to emptiness...it is impossible that God will fail to do his part by communicating Himself to it, at least silently and secretly."[15] Also: "As soon as natural things are driven out of the enamored soul, the divine are naturally and supernaturally infused, since there can be no void in nature."[16] This image is particularly forceful in our day. We are so familiar with vacuum-packed coffee cans. As soon as we puncture the lid, the outside atmosphere fills the void with a hiss of air rushing in. In a similar way, as soon as the soul becomes empty of natural things – sense knowledge, images, reasoning and affections – then the divine peace and calm of God's presence will be supernaturally infused to fill the emptiness for "there can be no void in nature"!

E. THE SUN EVER SHINING

Another of John's metaphors is that God is like the sun ever shining: "God, like the sun, stands above souls ready to communicate Himself. As the sun rises in the morning and shines upon your house,

---

14 DN, II, 9, 4.

15 LF, III, 46 (notice ftn. 7 on p. 23, indicating this section deals with beginning contemplation.)

16 A, II, 15, 4.

so that its light may enter if you open the shutters, so God...will enter the soul that is empty and fill it with divine goods."[17]

That is, just as the sun is ever shining high in the sky, so God is ever ready to shine in our souls once it is empty of clutter and clear of dust.

He explains that

> the principal agent...is God, who secretly and quietly inserts in the soul loving wisdom and knowledge, without specified acts.... Thus the individual should proceed only with a loving attention to God, without making specific acts. He should conduct himself passively...without efforts of his own, but with simple, loving awareness....[18]

We must be careful here to be totally realistic. According to John of the Cross, the beginning of contemplation is part of the illuminative way or the way of proficients.[19] But this is still the dark night in which the natural faculties of intellect and will are dark. Yet **God begins to communicate himself to us** by means of a quasi-experiential direct contact beyond all thought, so that God himself is experienced and tasted "silently and secretly" without clear understanding. In the beginning, this experience of God may be tenuous and slight; God may touch our intellect with divine light or inflame our will with love, but whatever form it takes, it is "an inflow of God into the soul...which the contemplatives call infused contemplation."[20] This is how we begin to experience God, the sun, communicating in a quasi-experiential direct

---

17   LF, II, 47 and 46 (note ftn. 7 on p. 23, indicating this section deal with the beginning of contemplation).

18   *Ibid.* 33.

19   Cf. DN, I, 1, 1; DN, II, 1, 1; SC, III, 47 and 46.

20   DN, II, 5, 1.

contact with us. In time, this experience will become more enlightening and more absorbing of our whole self, because of the comforting and loving presence of God.

F. AGENT, GUIDE AND MOVER

"In contemplation the activity of the senses and of discursive reflection terminates, and God alone is the agent and one Who then speaks secretly to the ...silent soul.... [T]he chief agent, guide and mover of souls in this matter [at the beginning of contemplation] ...is the Holy Spirit, Who is never neglectful of souls."[21] Here, John urges us not to rely on our own rational faculties and efforts, but rather on the infused wisdom of the Holy Spirit, who is "the principal agent, guide and mover" in all of contemplative prayer: "This communication [of dark contemplation] is secret and dark to the work of the intellect and the other faculties insofar as these faculties do not acquire it but the Holy Spirit infuses it and puts it in order in the soul."[22]

This reference to the Holy Spirit as "the principal agent, guide and mover" of souls seems to parallel the Gospel of John on the work of the Holy Spirit in all Jesus' disciples. As Jesus was about to leave his disciples, he promised that he would not leave them orphans but would send the Holy Spirit to be with them always: "I will not leave you orphans..."(Jo. 14, 18). "[M]y Father will love [you], and we will come to [you] and make our dwelling with [you]" (Jo. 14, 23) [in the person of our Spirit], "the Spirit of truth," who will "be with you always" (Jo. 14, 17, 16). My Spirit "will guide you to all truth" (Jo. 16, 13) and "teach you everything" (Jo. 14, 26). Here Jesus establishes the foundation for the entire work of the Holy Spirit in all his followers.

---

21 LF, III, 46 (note ftn. 7, p. 23, above, indicating that this section deals with beginning contemplation).

22 DN, II, 17, 2.

This Spirit dwells with them permanently as the new presence of Jesus in each one individually. The influence of the Holy Spirit is not limited to ordinary grace and prayer. Certainly this "everything" and "all truth" do not exclude infused contemplation.

Notice how well these promises of Jesus parallel John of the Cross' teaching about the Holy Spirit as "the agent and guide and mover of souls":

AGENT: "[The Father] will give you another Advocate to be with you always, the Spirit of truth" (14, 16-17).

GUIDE: "[T]he holy Spirit...will teach you everything" (14, 26) and "guide you to

all truth" (16, 13).

MOVER: "[T]he holy Spirit...will...remind you of all that [I] told you" (14, 26) and help you to carry it out.

John of the Cross assures us that God's Spirit will take over the active role of teacher and guide. We must now remain passive and peacefully aware of God's intimate presence. In this contemplative prayer, only God's Spirit is active, infusing a sense of God's presence and leading us to a direct knowledge and love of God.

PRAYING WITH JOHN'S IMAGES

These are some of the images that John offers us at the beginning of contemplation. His poems and commentaries of the *Spiritual Canticle* and *Living Flame* also offer endless metaphors for advanced contemplation (the unitive way). Hopefully, the images described in this chapter will stir up our imagination and engage our intellect in ways that are conducive to contemplation. Any one of them can be used either at the beginning of our prayer to help us focus our prayer, or within contemplation so that, despite our feeling empty and powerless, we can have confidence in the power of the Holy Spirit: "Little by little and very soon the divine peace and calm...will be infused into [your] soul.... Learn to be empty of all things – interiorly and exteriorly – and you will behold that I am God." [23]

Chapter 9
Practical Advice for the Beginning of Contemplation

John of the Cross gives a lot of practical advice for the beginning of contemplation in *Dark Night, Book I*. This whole book deals with the **passive night of senses**. In terms of our prayer, this passive night of senses consists essentially in our inability to meditate, because all our natural faculties are now darkened. To use John's terminology, this includes the bodily senses (seeing, hearing, touch, smell, taste), the interior bodily senses (imagination, and fancy), the faculties of the soul (concupiscence and irascibleness), the desires or affections (joy, hope, fear, grief) and the spiritual faculties (memory, intellect, will). Modern psychology would have different names for many of these and would add to the list.

This very inability to meditate, the darkness of these senses and the void in our intellect and will are the necessary conditions for the new form of prayer that God is beginning to bestow. John insists that this new way of prayer is properly called contemplation:

> [A] person should not mind if the operations of his faculties are being lost to him; he ought to desire rather that this be done quickly so that he may be no obstacle to the operation of the infused contemplation which God is bestowing...and make room in his spirit for the enkindling and burning of love that this dark and secret contemplation bears and communicates to his soul. For contemplation is nothing else than a secret and peaceful and loving inflow of God....[1]

---

1   DN, I, 10, 6.

John wants us to know that this dark prayer is actually the beginning of contemplation:

> This food is the beginning of a contemplation that is dark and dry to the senses.... [N]ow in this state of contemplation, when the soul has left discursive meditation and entered the state of proficients, it is God who works in it.... At this time a person's own efforts are of no avail....[2]

That is, this prayer is not just a period of transition between meditation and contemplation nor a proximate preparation for contemplation; rather it is the **very beginning of contemplation:**

> At the time of the aridities of this sensory night, God [withdraws] the soul from the life of the senses and [places] it in that of the spirit – that is, he brings it from meditation to contemplation – where the soul no longer has the power to work or meditate with its faculties on the things of God.[3]

He teaches that this is actually something new in the soul, **a new experience;** it is not simply a deepening of what has gone before, not just a continuation and further simplifying of meditation. We have seen our own personal activity in meditation become more simple and even reduced to nothing. The old world of our senses and intellectual ideas is now remote and useless. We no longer meditate by means of ideas, images or affections. Now God begins to act, though darkly. God almost imperceptibly infuses himself into our soul and awakens a new level of awareness. This is the actual beginning of contemplation.

---

2   *Ibid.* 9, 6-7.
3   *Ibid.* 10, 1.

We experience this night of contemplation as darkness, because we have only an undefined intimation of God's presence. The experience itself is ineffable, for it is void of any intermediary of sense or image.

The critical point, that John of the Cross often repeats, is that this dark, passive and simple form of prayer is truly contemplation:

> ...in this state of contemplation, when the soul has left discursive meditation and entered the state of proficients, it is God who works in it. He therefore binds the interior faculties and leaves no support in the intellect, nor satisfaction in the will, nor remembrance in the memory.... At this time God does not communicate Himself through the senses as he did before...but begins to communicate Himself through pure spirit by an act of simple contemplation, in which there is no discursive succession of thought.[4]

John takes great care in repeating just what this beginning of contemplation consists in, because it is not what most people understand it to be. They hear about more advanced forms of contemplation such as raptures, ecstasies and visions. They do not understand that those are not usually the experiences at the beginning of contemplation. They do not realize that their natural progression of prayer – from meditation to affective prayer to simpler prayer – leads them to this very next step. They see their own personal activity reduced to nothing; their reflections, personal affections and quiet insights have mostly disappeared; God no longer seems to touch them through ideas, images or affections. They find themselves in front of a wall without any satisfying thoughts and they wonder, "Where did I go wrong?"

---

4   DN, I, 9, 7-8. See also: DN, II, 5, 1 and 3.

John wants us to know that this troubling development is not a dead end, not a wall at all. It is actually the natural development of our prayer and the necessary condition for God to act in us in a new way.[5] As long as we had filled our minds with all our rational ideas, images, reasoning and affections, there was no room for a new and infused way of experiencing God. Only when we admit that all our rational efforts can take us no farther, are we willing to let God take over and to be peaceful and attentive in that dark night. Then God begins to act and show his presence, though obscurely. God almost imperceptibly infuses himself into our soul and awakens us to a new level of awareness. God opens a new door for us. At first, we experience this as darkness because the experience itself is so subtle and elusive. In addition, we have no words to describe this; we use words such as "know, see, feel, sense, perceive, touch," but they are not adequate to express how we experience God now; they are only metaphors or analogies. The experience itself is ineffable, for it is void of any intermediaries of sense or image. But this direct inflow of God is actually the beginning of contemplation. Over a period of time, this new way of experiencing God will gradually reach some degree of clarity. Only little by little does this gleam in the night seem closer and somewhat distinct. God only increases his light according to our ability and our faithfulness in this way.

As we have already noted, John of the Cross' advice for those who can no longer meditate and are beginning contemplation is entirely clear and simple:

---

5   DN, II, 16, 4: "Even if God were to give these faculties the activity and delight of supernatural, divine things, they would be unable to receive it except in their own way, very basely and naturally. As the philosopher says, whatever is received is received according to the mode of the receiver.... Thus all these faculties and appetites of the soul are tempered and prepared for the sublime reception...of the divine and supernatural, which is unreceivable until the old man dies."

The attitude necessary in the night of sense is to pay no attention to discursive meditation, since this is not the time for it. They should allow the soul to remain in rest and quietude, even though it may seem very obvious to them that they are doing nothing and wasting time.... They must be content simply with a **loving and peaceful attentiveness to God** and live without the concern, without the effort, and without the desire to taste or feel Him.[6]

John insists here, that once we can no longer meditate with sensible images, imaginations, rational thoughts and affections, we should not continue to struggle with our natural faculties but "remain in rest and quietude" with "a loving and peaceful attentiveness to God." Very simply, we should remain peaceful and attentive in God's presence.

Again and again he assures us that the primary agent in this contemplative prayer is God:

...the principal agent [now]...is God, who secretly and quietly inserts in the soul loving wisdom and knowledge, without specific acts.... Thus the individual also should proceed only with a loving attention to God, without making specific acts. He should conduct himself passively...without efforts of his own, but with simple, loving awareness....[7]

That is, all our activity can be summed up in this one word: **attentive.** Since the natural operations of our intellect and will are totally helpless to attain the direct knowledge of God, all we can do is put them at rest. Only when we put to rest all our sensible ways of knowing, will there be room for this direct, infused experience of God.

---

6   DN, I, 10, 4 (emphasis added).

7   LF, III, 33.

Our whole effort is to remain quiet, peaceful, open and receptive to this new experience.

METAPHORS THAT HELP US BE RECEPTIVE

At the beginning of prayer, we can learn to be open, attentive and receptive by considering various metaphors.

1. There is nothing we can do to water this garden; we can no longer even bring up buckets from the well of meditation. We have no control over the rainwater that comes from God's infused contemplation. 2. We need a new way of breathing in this rarified air; only the pure oxygen of God will sustain us at this altitude. 3. We are beyond our ability to swim any more; all we can do is float in the water and wait for God to carry us along. 4. All our efforts cannot open this door to the new experience of God; the most we can do is remove all the obstacles of our mental images and rational thoughts. 5. God is the sun ever shining; he will certainly shine in our soul once it is empty of the clutter of sensible images and natural reasoning. And these same metaphors may help us to be patient in this passive form of prayer – content to be peaceful and attentive in God's presence.

Thomas Green offers another image that might help us to be open, attentive and receptive in our prayer. It is that of floating in water:

> ...floating [is not difficult] because it demands much skill but because it demands much letting go. The secret of floating is in learning not to do all the things we instinctively want to do. We must rest on the water as on a pillow, we don't sink; we float![8]

This whole experience of beginning contemplation is the Lord's

---

8   Thomas Green, S.J., *When the Well Runs Dry* (Notre Dame, IN: Ave Maria Press, 1979), p 143.

way of making floaters out of swimmers. He wants us to trust him enough to relax, to surrender to the dark water; He wants us to believe that our floating is not to be directionless, getting us to want to keep ourselves rigid, ready to save ourselves the moment a big wave comes along.... If we can persuade ourselves to put our heads back, breathe slowly and let ourselves drift, we will let him hold us up and lead us where he wills. He has a goal in mind and will lead us to it.

SUGGESTION FOR PRAYER

When we reach this dark night of the senses, we can feel lost in our prayer, because all our faculties are dark and all our efforts are useless. Despite the guidance of John of the Cross, we would like to have some example of just how to proceed in this beginning of contemplative prayer. Here is one example.

Receive, O Lord, my whole freedom – my senses, my imagination, my affections, my reasonings. All these faculties I have received from you. I renounce the use of all of them during this prayer, unless it be according to your will. Grant me only the inspiration of your Spirit, nothing more.

Lord, I am content to dwell in this dark night in which all my faculties are helpless. This darkness is my friend, for only in this night can your new light become visible; this silence is the way to wisdom, for only in complete quiet can the gentle voice of your Spirit be heard; this helplessness is the only way forward, for you will carry me where I am unable to go; this emptiness is the way to fullness, for the more I acknowledge this void, the more you prepare to fill it; this weakness is my strength, for only when I know that I am nothing and you are God, will you give me your power.

I rely on the promises of Jesus: "I will not leave you orphans" (Jo. 14, 18). "[M]y Father will love [you], and we will come to [you] and make our dwelling with [you]" (Jo. 14, 23) [in the person of our Spirit], "the Spirit of truth" who will "be with you always" (Jo. 14, 17, 16). My Spirit "will guide you to all truth" (Jo. 16, 13) and "teach you everything" (Jo. 14, 26).

So I remain at peace in this gentle night for "[T]he love of God has been poured out into [my heart] through the holy Spirit that has been given to [me]" (Rom. 5, 5). I believe in your Spirit of Jesus present within me. This Spirit is the permanent assurance of your love and my guide in the way of truth. You ask only that I be attentive and receptive to your presence and guidance. My attitude in this beginning of contemplation is to be peaceful and attentive to your loving presence. I am profoundly confident in this dark and simple prayer, for "[H]ow much more will the Father in heaven give the holy Spirit to those who ask him?" (Lk. 11, 13).

* * * * *

If you wish, you can start your time of contemplation with any of these suggestions. But the heart of our prayer and most of our time should be spent in a peaceful and attentive remaining in God's presence. At first our sense of the presence of God may be tenuous and slight; in time it will become more perceptible; eventually it will be more and more absorbing of our whole self.

We may wonder what is the content of this contemplative prayer. Clearly it is not a new, private revelation; we already know the whole of revelation by our faith. What we discover about God's great actions and mysteries in contemplation is not a deeper theological understanding, but an experience of the presence of God in a closer intimacy. If we can speak at all of the content of contemplative prayer, it is an experience of God deep within us, along with an infused sense of his goodness and love. We do not look for intellectual clarity or theological insight, but for an intimate absorption in love. John of the Cross is most consistent with his advice to us:

> When the spiritual person cannot meditate, he should learn to remain in God's presence with a loving attention and tranquil intellect, even though he seems to himself to be idle. For little by little and very soon the divine calm and peace...will be infused into his soul.... Learn to be empty of all things – interiorly and exteriorly – and you will behold that I am God.[9]

The next two chapters will offer various ways to help us follow his counsel.

---

9   A, II, 15, 5.

Chapter 10
From Paradox to Insight

In all of John of the Cross' works, there is one unique paragraph that is critical for our understanding of his entire teaching about the beginning of contemplation. This one paragraph, one triple paradox, gives us an insight into his central teaching on contemplation and will act as an outline for this chapter:

> [E]ven though this happy night [of contemplation] darkens the spirit, it does so only to impart light...; and even though it humbles a person and reveals his miseries, it does so only to exalt him; and even though it impoverishes and empties him of all...natural affections, it does so only that he may reach out divinely to the enjoyment of all earthly and heavenly things.[1]

John is teaching here about the passive dark night of the spirit or contemplation. He presents three paradoxes: darkness leads to light; lowliness leads to rising up; and emptiness leads to fullness. He wants us to know that contemplation darkens, humbles and empties our soul **only** to enlighten, to exalt and to fill the soul. Once we gain insight into this one central teaching, we will be able to understand the heart of John's teaching on the practice of contemplation.

A. JOHN'S COUNSEL FOR THOSE WHO ARE AT THE THRESHOLD OF CONTEMPLATION

We will begin our study of this central paradox with John's teaching for "proficients, at the beginning of their entry into...con-

---

1   DN, II, 9, 1.

templation."[2] Here John is counseling those who have been practicing discursive meditation but now often find they are void of sensible images, imaginings, affections and reasoning. He has just described his famous three signs for **discontinuing** discursive meditation: 1) one often or regularly cannot make discursive meditation; 2) one is disinclined to concentrate on sensible objects or ideas; 3) one is inclined to remain alone in loving attention on God even though the experience is subtle and delicate. Today, that group of people would include many who are practicing simple prayer or the prayer of presence or centering prayer or praying with a sacred word or mantra. John gives a general description of what is sometimes or often experienced by people who pray in these ways:

> [A]t the beginning of this state the loving knowledge [of God] is almost unnoticeable. There are two reasons for this: first, the incipient loving knowledge is extremely subtle and delicate, and almost imperceptible; second, a person who is habituated to the exercise of meditation, which is wholly sensible, hardly perceives or feels this new insensible, purely spiritual experience.[3]

In this *Ascent of Mount Carmel, Book II,* John is counseling those who are at the very threshold of contemplation or who occasionally practice contemplation. **First,** he assures them that this darkness leads to light: "As soon as natural things are driven out of the enamored soul, the divine are naturally and supernaturally infused, since there can be no void in nature."[4] Here John teaches that as soon as natural thoughts and sensible images no longer occupy us in prayer,

---

2   A, II, 15, chapter title and paragraph 1.
3   *Ibid.* 13, 7.
4   *Ibid.* 15, 4.

God will infuse his supernatural light into us. He assures us that once a natural void is created, it will be filled with the infused action of God. This image of filling the void seems particularly forceful in our day. We are so familiar with vacuum-packed coffee cans and know that as soon as we puncture the lid, the outside atmosphere fills the void with a hiss of air rushing in. In a similar way, once our prayer becomes dark or empty of all sensible images, God will fill the void with his infused grace – though the light may only be "extremely subtle and delicate" for a while.

Second, John assures them that God humbles the soul only to exalt it:

> If a person will eliminate these impediments...voiding himself of all forms and apprehensible images...and live in pure nakedness and poverty of spirit...his soul in its simplicity and purity will then be immediately transformed into simple and pure Wisdom....[5]

That is, because the soul can no longer pray with the sensible images and insights of discursive meditation, it recognizes its own inability and poverty of spirit. But God will soon instruct it with his own wisdom in contemplation and so raise it up.

Third, John assures them that emptiness leads to fullness:

> When the spiritual person cannot meditate, he should learn to remain in God's presence...even though he seems to himself to be idle. For little by little and very soon...a wondrous, sublime knowledge of God...will be infused into his soul.... Learn to

---

5   *Idem*

be empty of all things – interiorly and exteriorly – and you will behold that I am God.[6]

For John, emptiness of all sensible images, rational thoughts and affections is required so that God might freely communicate himself to the soul. He promises that God will not fail to do his part and bring the soul to enjoy a new way of experiencing him.

Note that all his counsel here deals with those who are at the threshold of contemplation. That is, they have reached the point where discursive meditation has become dark and empty. At times, they may experience the beginning of contemplation, but it may be slight and subtle in the early stages.

What does all this mean for all of us who are in this stage of prayer? John wants us to know that this dark and empty prayer is filled with promise.

- He assures us that we can be **content** in such dark and unsatisfying prayer, for "there can be no void in nature." He means that the very darkness is the necessary condition for God's supernatural way of acting in our prayer.
- And we can be **peaceful** even though we can no longer pray with the insights and affections we experienced in discursive meditation. Just because we are convinced of our "lowliness and misery: and find "no satisfaction in self," God esteems this lack of self-satisfaction and is ready to instruct us in his wisdom.
- And we can be **confident** even though we are empty and helpless, because such emptiness of sensible images, rational thoughts and affections is required for God to communicate

---

6   *Ibid.* 15, 5.

himself to us. "Learn to be empty of all things...and you will behold that I am God."

B. JOHN'S COUNSEL FOR THOSE WHO ARE BEGINNING TO PRACTICE CONTEMPLATION

In *The Dark Night, Book II,* John explains **why** this dark night of contemplation must first darken, humble and empty the soul before it can enlighten, exalt and fill the soul.

[T]he affections, sentiments and apprehensions [of contemplation] are of another sort and are so eminent and so different from [those experienced naturally in discursive meditation] that their...possession demands the annihilation and expulsion of the natural affections and apprehensions; **for two contraries cannot coexist in one subject**. Hence...this dark night of contemplation must necessarily annihilate it first and undo it in its lowly ways by putting it in darkness, dryness, conflict, and emptiness. For the light imparted to the soul...transcends all natural light and which does not belong naturally to the intellect.[7]

His argument is straightforward: "two contraries cannot exist in one subject" at the same time. Therefore, "this dark night of contemplation must necessarily...undo [the soul] in its lowly ways by putting it in darkness...and emptiness. For the [divine] light transcends all natural light." That is, the normal way for our intellect to operate is by means of sensible objects, but in contemplation God affects the soul directly, without sensible images.

---

7   DN, II, 9, 2 (emphasis added).

A few chapters later John describes his **first paradox**: this darkness leads to light:

> [W]hen you see your...faculties incapacitated for any interior exercise, do not be afflicted; think of this as a grace, since God is freeing you from yourself ...[so that now] God takes you by the hand and guides you in darkness, as though you were blind, along a way and to a place you do not know.[8]

And he adds immediately that you will succeed "in reaching this place." That is, as above in footnote 7, "the light imparted to the soul...transcends all natural light."

The **second paradox** is: in contemplation, God humbles the soul in order to exalt it. John insists that this humility and poverty of spirit leads to exaltation by God:

> [T]he soul must first be set in emptiness and poverty of spirit.... Thus empty, it is truly poor...and thereby able to live that new and blessed life which is the state of union with God, attained by means of this night.[9]

That is, humility and "poverty of spirit" will lead to this state of union with God that is our exaltation.

The **third paradox** is that emptiness leads to fullness. The best quote for this is found in the *Living Flame,* in the one long section where he focuses on those who are beginning contemplation.[10]

---

8   *Ibid.* 16, 7.

9   *Ibid.* 9, 4.

10   LF, III, paragraphs 30-62. Throughout this section, John of the Cross is instructing spiritual directors how to help those who are beginning to practice contemplation, when "God begins to wean the soul...and place it in the state of contemplation."

When the soul frees itself of all things and attains to emptiness...
concerning them, which is equivalent to what it can do of itself,
it is impossible that God fail to do his part by communicating
Himself to it, at least secretly and silently.[11]

Here John guarantees that as long as the soul is empty and passive, God will do his part soon and without fail. So though the soul is
passive and empty, it can be entirely confident because his emptiness
will result in God's presence and light.

What does all this mean for us as we begin to practice contemplation? John's answer is found in the central quote we are focused
on in this chapter:

[E]ven though this happy night darkens the spirit, it does so
only to impart light...; and even though it humbles a person and
reveals his miseries, it does so only to exalt him; and even though
it impoverishes and empties him of all...natural affections, it
does so only that he may reach out divinely to the enjoyment of
all earthly and heavenly things....[12]

In part A above, when John was speaking about those on the
threshold of contemplation who simply could no longer pray with
discursive meditation, he assured them that even then this natural
stage of prayer is filled with promise, for such dark and empty prayer
is the necessary condition for God's supernatural way of acting in our
prayer. He wants them to know, even then, that as soon as they create
this natural void, God will soon fill that void with his presence.

---

11   *Idem.* 46.

12   DN, II, 9, 1.

But now his counsel is for those who are actually **beginning to practice contemplation**. And his counsel is clearly parallel to that earlier stage of prayer. But here the darkness and emptiness are not just natural effects of ordinary prayer. Rather, **the very nature of contemplation** is such that it increases the darkness and emptiness in three ways: 1) this dark night "darkens the spirit," so that no sensible objects or thoughts can occupy the mind or distract it; 2) it "humbles a person" with a sense of its own incapacity and poverty of spirit; 3) it "empties him of all natural affections for material things. Nevertheless, John calls this a **"happy night"** for the very darkness prepares us to be more receptive to God's light, and our sense of poverty and incapacity inclines us to be more open to God's power, and our emptiness makes us realize that we can only passively await God's fullness.

The second part of these three counsels is entirely positive and filled with promise. He tells us that the purpose of this darkness is **only** to impart light; the purpose of this sense of lowliness is **only** to exalt us; the purpose of emptiness is **only** to fill us with God's presence. Or to use the words of the above quotes:

- The purpose of the darkness of contemplation is so that God can take us by the hand and impart a light that "transcends all natural light."
- And the purpose of the poverty of spirit is that then God can raise us up to a new union with him.
- And the purpose of the emptiness we feel in terms of all we can do by our ordinary prayer is so that God may do his part "by communicating himself to [us], at least secretly and silently."

This is the genius of John of the Cross' counsel for us at the beginning of contemplation. This triple paradox permits us to be **content in the darkness**, because that is the necessary condition for God's supernatural light; we can be **peaceful in our poverty of spirit** for "there can be no void in nature," no vacuum in supernature; we can be **confident in our emptiness** for "it is impossible that God fail to do his part by communicating himself to [us], at least secretly and silently."

SUGGESTION FOR PRAYER

Lord, I believe that even though you have brought me to this darkness, you do so only to give light. For only when I experience my blindness, Can I turn to you for a new and greater source of light.

I believe that even though you humble me, so that all my natural faculties are of no avail in prayer, you do so only to exalt me. For only when I experience my lowliness, can I exalt in your gracious infusion of grace.

I believe that even though you empty me, so that all my natural resources add up to nothing, you do so only to fill me. For only when I experience this void, can I know that all power comes only from you.

You have taught me that all these experiences have only **one purpose**: to prepare me for contemplation. With John of the Cross, in contemplation, I can admit my lowliness, my darkness and my emptiness, for that is the sure way to be filled with your supernatural light and grace. This is just what John of the Cross makes clear: "As soon as natural things are driven out of the enamored soul, the divine are naturally and supernaturally infused, since there can be no void in nature.[13] And even more insistently: "When the soul frees itself from all things...it is impossible that God should fail to do his part by com-

---

13 A, II, 15, 4.
14 LF, III, 46 (note ftn. 7, p. 23, above, indicating this section deals with beginning contemplation).

municating Himself to it, at least secretly and silently."[14] I know that this spiritual poverty and emptiness is not only a condition for your contemplative grace; their only purpose is to raise up, give light and fill me with your new presence and light.

Chapter 11
The Content of Contemplation

Even though John of the Cross is quite clear and practical about how we should act during our time of prayer, we are still left with one troublesome question: What is the actual **content** of contemplation? It is one thing to describe contemplation negatively by saying it does not include sense images, affections, imaginations or reasonings, but how can we describe contemplation positively? What do we positively experience in this new form of prayer infused by God? The best answer I can give is by means of John of the Cross' descriptions of the four forms of God's direct inflowing in contemplation. He describes these forms especially in chapter 13 of his *Dark Night, II* and in stanza III, numbers 46-49 of the *Living Flame*. Regarding his teaching in the *Living Flame*, we note that here John is offering counsel to spiritual directors who are guiding people just beginning contemplation. In numbers 30 to 62 of stanza III, John focuses on one situation: "[W]hen God begins to wean the soul...and place it in the state of contemplation.... [T]he principal agent...is God.... [The individual] should conduct himself passively."[1] So quoting from this section is entirely valid for our topic, the beginning of contemplation.

The first form is a quasi-experiential **direct contact with God** beyond all thought, in which God himself is experienced and tasted without clear understanding or love. John affirms: "God [communicates] Himself to [the soul] at least secretly and silently."[2] Thomas Merton defines contemplation in this way: "[P]ure contemplation...is a direct,

---

1   LF, III, 32. He tells spiritual directors here, "[D]irectors should not impose meditation upon persons in this state.... The individual...should proceed only with a loving attention on God, without making specific acts."

2   DN, I, 10, 4.

quasi experiential contact with God beyond all thought, that is to say without the medium of concepts."[3] That is, God begins to act and show his presence, though obscurely. God almost imperceptibly infuses himself into our soul and awakens a new level of awareness of his presence.

The second form is that of an esteem and desire for God, an urgent **longing of love** in **the will,** without intellectual understanding. While it is true that in natural operations our will can only love what the intellect understands, in contemplation God can infuse his love directly into the soul without knowledge in the intellect: "[G]od...can inflame the will with a touch of the warmth of his love even though the intellect does not understand."[4] John explains that in the beginning of contemplation the will and affections are more often inflamed than the intellect: "It is more common to experience the touch of burning in the will than the touch of understanding in the intellect...."[5]

The third form of contemplation is the communication of **mystical knowledge to the intellect**. Sometimes God touches the intellect with divine light and understanding, so that the intellect now understands by means of divine wisdom infused by God: "Through this contemplation, God teaches the soul secretly and instructs it... without its doing anything nor understanding how this happens."[6] That is, sometimes contemplation communicates mystical knowledge to the intellect while leaving the will in dryness, without the actual union of love.

Later, in the *Living Flame,* John notes that "[S]ometimes...God... communicates Himself to one faculty more than the other; sometimes

---

3   Thomas Merton, *The Inner Experience,* (NY: HarperCollins, 2003), p. 68.
4   LF, III, 49.
5   DN, II, 13, 2.
6   *Ibid.* 5, 1.

more knowledge is experienced than love, and at other times more love than knowledge, and likewise at times all knowledge is felt without love, or all love without any knowledge."[7]

The fourth form of contemplation mentioned at this stage is that which **acts upon the intellect and will together**:

> Sometimes...this contemplation acts upon the intellect and will together and sublimely, tenderly and forcibly enkindles love. ...once the intellect is more purged, these two faculties are sometimes united; and in the measure they are both purged, this union becomes so much more perfect and deeper in quality."[8]

These four forms give us some sense of the content of contemplation in the early stages. It should be noted that here, as in all of contemplation, we are not speaking about a new, private revelation; we already know the whole of revelation by our faith. What we discover about God's great actions and mysteries in contemplation is not the revelation of some new item of theology but an experience of the presence of God in a closer intimacy. If we can speak at all of the **content** of contemplative prayer, it is an experience of God deep within us, accompanied at times with an infused sense of God's goodness and love. We do not look for intellectual clarity or theological insight but for an intimate absorption in God. In the early stages of contemplation, the experience itself is usually quite subtle and elusive. But over a period of time, this new way of experiencing God will gradually reach some degree of clarity. God only increases his light according to our ability and faithfulness in this way. As John defines

7   LF, III, 49 (note ftn. 7, p. 23, above).

8   DN, II, 12, 2.

it: "[C]ontemplation is nothing else than a sacred and peaceful and loving inflow of God, which...fires the soul in the spirit of love...."[9]

SUGGESTION FOR PRAYER

One way for us to be open, attentive and receptive in contemplation is to begin with these words of the Johannine Jesus;

> "[T]he Father...will give you another Advocate to be with you always, the Spirit of truth.... I will not leave you orphans; I will come to you [in the person of the Spirit].... The Advocate, the holy Spirit...will teach you everything and remind you of all that [I] told you...[and] guide you to all truth." (Jo. 14, 16-18, 26; 16, 13).

Lord, what you were to the apostles, your Spirit is to be for me now. I believe that your Spirit is now present within me as my permanent teacher and guide in following you and in prayer. I will do nothing now but rest in this darkness and be attentive to his inspiration. On my own, I am empty and powerless. Yet I am most confident because of your Spirit of wisdom and love, who is my advocate and guide. For the Spirit will teach me everything and guide me to all truth by enlightening me in a completely new way. Your Spirit will lead me to a knowledge and love of God without images and reasoning, without intermediaries. With your Spirit, I am willing to be empty of all natural things and still be guided to all truth.

---

9   DN, I, 10, 6,

Chapter 12
God's Part in Contemplation

If the content of contemplation involves God's infusion of himself directly into our soul, we still want to know what actually brings this about, what prepares us for this new experience. We can begin with John's terminology for contemplation; he calls it a **passive dark night.** It is a night because all the natural faculties of the soul are dark and empty; it is passive because all the action comes from God; it is contemplation because it is the direct inflowing of God in the soul. In his words:

> [God] leaves the intellect in darkness, the will in aridity, the memory in emptiness and the affections in supreme affliction... by depriving the soul of the feeling and satisfaction it previously obtained from spiritual blessings. For this privation is one of the conditions required that the spiritual form, which is the union of love, may be introduced in the spirit....The Lord works all of this in the soul by means of a pure and dark contemplation....[1]

John insists that this is something new in the soul, a **new experience**; it is not simply a deepening of what has gone before, not just a continuation and further simplifying of the active prayer of faith; this is the beginning of infused contemplation. We have seen our own personal activity reduced to nothing. Now God begins to act; he begins to show his presence, though obscurely. He no longer touches us through ideas, images, or affections; now he communicates directly, though tenuously. The old world of our senses is now remote

---

1   DN, II, 3, 3. Cf. *ibid.* 16, 1.

and useless; God almost imperceptibly infuses himself into our soul; he awakens us to a new level of awareness. He opens a new door in the center of our being that is free of variety, complexity, and multiplicity; we reach the simple reality of God himself.

We experience this as darkness because, at first, we only have an undefined intimation of God's presence; the experience itself is so subtle and elusive. In addition, we have no words to describe this new activity of God; we use verbs such as "know, see, feel, sense, perceive and touch"; but they are not adequate for expressing how we experience God now; they serve only as metaphors or analogies. The experience itself is ineffable, for it is void of any intermediaries of sense or image.

God's action prepares us for a new kind of wisdom. In order to do that, God first brings us to a clear sense of our helplessness and emptiness. This complete darkness of mind, this total inability for any kind of discursive meditation, leads us naturally to be open and receptive to God. For only when we are completely aware of our own emptiness, are we inclined to God's new way of wisdom. In the beginning of this passive night, God's work is mostly negative, helping to empty the soul that he may then be free to illumine it. In this beginning of contemplation, God only prepares the soul for his illumination.

Notice the various connections that John makes between this darkness of our own faculties and God's beginning to illumine us with his new and infused wisdom.

Thus, he teaches that it is **fitting** that the darkness of our natural faculties should last as long as necessary: "It is fitting that this darkness last as long as is necessary for the annihilation of the intellect's way of understanding...that the divine illumination take place."[2] He adds that

---

2   DN, II, 9, 3.

once our natural operations cease to act in their ordinary manner, they will **soon** be given the ability to receive the infused knowledge of God: "God...never mortifies but to give life , nor humbles but to exalt.... Which favor will be granted a short time afterwards."[3] Finally, the void or vacuum that is affected here in the natural faculties **leads to fullness**: "As soon as natural things are driven out...the divine are naturally and supernaturally infused, since there can be no void in nature."[4] That is, this natural void leads to divine fullness – the infusion of God's wisdom.

What we need to be completely convinced of now, is that this new way of contemplation is God's work alone; we can do nothing. God's presence will be imperceptible for some time in this new experience. God may give us grant a sense of peace and calm; he may communicate his presence at least secretly and silently. But the experience may be tenuous and slight at first. In time it will become perceptible, as a comforting and loving presence. Over a long period of time, this new way of knowing God will gradually reach some degree of clarity. In a word, we need time to become accustomed to this new and direct way of knowing God. Then we will approach prayer gladly, as if going to meet an intimate friend. The next chapter, the Tranquil Night, will try to describe this next stage of contemplation.

SUGGESTION FOR PRAYER

Recall here John's practical advice for us as we learn to depend on God's new way of acting:

...the principal agent [now]...is God, who secretly and quietly inserts in the soul loving wisdom and knowledge, without

---

3   *Ibid.* 23, 10.
4   A, II, 15, 4.

specific acts....Thus the individual also should proceed only with a loving attention to God, without making specific acts. He should conduct himself passively...without efforts of his own, but with the simple, loving awareness....[5]

All our activity can be summed up in this one word: **attentive**. Since the natural operations of our intellect and will are totally helpless to attain the direct knowledge of God, all we can do is put them at rest; we try to remain quiet, peaceful, serene, at rest; our only effort is to be lovingly attentive, open, receptive. In John's Gospel, Jesus hints at one way of being trusting and receptive: "[T]he Father...will give you another Advocate to be with you always, the Spirit of truth" (14, 16-17). "[H]e will guide you to all truth" (16, 13) and "will teach you everything" (14, 26), in the way of prayer.

Lord, what you were to the apostles, your Spirit is to be for me now. I believe that your Spirit is now present within me as my friend, my teacher, my guide in following you. I can do nothing now but rest peacefully in this darkness, and be attentive to his inspiration. I am blind, deaf, mute, empty, helpless. Yet I am most confident, because of your Spirit of wisdom and love who is my advocate and guide. For he will "guide [me] to all truth" by enlightening me in a completely new way. The old way of images, reasonings and affections can go no farther. Now your Spirit will lead me on to the knowledge of God without intermediaries.

Spirit of God, be the breath of life for me now. I cannot breathe in this rare air without your help. I stand before this dark door; only you can open the door to a whole new world of God's knowledge and love.

---

5   LF, III, 33 (note ftn. 7, p. 23, above).

As St. Paul assures all of us: "[T]he Spirit...comes to the aid of our weakness; for we do not know how to pray as we ought, but the Spirit...intercedes with inexpressible groanings"(Rom. 8, 26). So, I will remain here, peaceful and at rest, simply attentive and receptive to your light.

*   *   *   *   *

The one thing we need to learn now is that this is God's work alone; we can do nothing. The images mentioned can impress this one norm on our mind constantly. Jesus' teaching about our new guide, the Holy Spirit, is our profound source of confidence. We can start our time of contemplation with any of these helps. But the heart of our prayer and most of our time should be spent in quiet and peaceful receptiveness. God's presence will be imperceptible for some time, as we begin to contemplate. Only gradually will we perceive the gleam of his presence. At first it will be tenuous and slight; only in time will it become perceptible. It will not become clear and visible, but it will be a comforting and loving presence. Then we will approach prayer gladly, as if going to meet an intimate friend.

Chapter 13
Passive, Attentive, and Confident

Again and again, we have repeated the one and only counsel of John of the Cross for those who are at the early stages of contemplation: that they be attentive. When we try to follow this simple counsel, we may find that merely being open, attentive and receptive in prayer leaves us feeling helpless and empty. We may wonder how this can be a positive and effective way to approach God. We feel the urge to ask where this will get us. John assures us that once we have emptied ourselves of all our natural discursive thoughts and thus created a natural void, we can expect God to do his part and grant us a new and supernatural experience of God's presence. This simple answer is expressed in so many different ways in John's writings. Here are four principal expressions of this simple answer. Each answer encourages us to admit our helplessness, while still being supremely confident that this will lead to God's infusion of contemplation.

First, in the *Ascent of Mount Carmel, Book II,* John speaks to "proficients (those whom God begins to place in this supernatural knowledge of contemplation)"[1] He tells them that if they cannot meditate, they "should learn to remain in God's presence with a loving attention and a tranquil intellect.... Learn to be empty of all things – interiorly and exteriorly – and you will behold that I am God."[2] That is, being empty of all things is a **necessary condition** for God's action. In John's terminology, he tells us that this active night of spirit (which is the topic of book II of the *Ascent*) leads to contemplation. In other words, when we are not occupied with our own natural thoughts

---

1   A, II, 15, 1.
2   *Ibid.* 2.

and are merely open, attentive and receptive, we have the required condition for God to freely act in us.

Second, in the same chapter, John instills an even greater confidence: "As soon as natural things are driven out of the enamored soul, the divine are naturally and supernaturally infused, since there can be **no void in nature**."[3] Here John assures us that as soon as natural things are driven out in our prayer, God will supernaturally infuse his presence, because once the natural void is created, the new and infused action of God will fill that void. That is, the void will be filled by God.

Third, in the *Dark Night, Book II,* John explains that this passive dark night leads naturally to a new kind of knowledge: "Even though this happy night darkens the spirit, it does so only to impart light."[4] He means that the **singular purpose** for this dark night of emptiness is that God may fill the soul with light. In the context, he argues that "two contraries cannot coexist in one subject,"[5] meaning that "this contemplation must first...annihilate [the intellect] of its natural light...that the divine light may...take its place."[6] The precise sequence of either darkness leading to light or light driving out darkness becomes reasonable because of John's point just above: "there can be no void in nature." We might ask a further question: how can the purpose of the darkness be ONLY to impart light? We might recall the discussion in chapter 4 about providence. Thus, we may exclusively see God's direct hand in this darkness/light. Or we may conclude that our effort to empty the intellect of all natural thoughts, is the very condition for God's grace to be free and unobstructed.

---

3   *Ibid.* 4.
4   DN, II, 9, 1.
5   *Ibid.* 2.
6   *Ibid.* 3.

Finally, in the *Living Flame,* when John is speaking about the beginning of contemplation,[7] he insists that once the soul "frees itself of all things," God will certainly communicate himself to it: "When the soul frees itself of all things and attains to emptiness...concerning them, which is equivalent to what it can do of itself, it is impossible that God fail to do his part by communicating Himself to it, at least secretly and silently."[8] When John asserts "**it is impossible that God fail to do his part,**" he guarantees that God will do his part as long as the soul is empty.

What these four insights teach us is that once we have created this void of all our sense images, ideas, imaginations, feelings and reasonings, we can expect God to do his part soon and without fail. Our confidence comes not from our merit, goodness or achievements, but from the promises of Christ to send the Spirit of God to teach us everything and to guide us in the way of truth. For, according to John of the Cross, this emptiness and void is the necessary condition for God's action and has only one purpose: to lead, to fill our soul with a new experience and light. He even guarantees that God will do his part by communicating himself to us, because there can be no void in nature, no vacuum in prayer.

SUGGESTION FOR PRAYER

.   Lord, I am content to be open, attentive and receptive in this prayer. It is right that I should be passive and helpless, void and empty. Such a condition has a singular purpose: to fill my soul with your presence. In fact, this is the necessary condition for me to behold

---

7   In LF, III, 44 –46, John focuses on those who are beginning contemplation as he notes in 44: "...since the soul has already...come to the way of the spirit, which is contemplation."

8   *Idem.* 46.

that you are God, directly present within me. I believe in the guarantee that you will do your part by communicating yourself to me without the intermediary of any sensible knowledge, because there can be no void in nature.

Lord, just because I am in this night that is void of natural light, there is no obstacle to your new light. So I am, finally, confident and really **open** to your infused light. And just because I am empty of any thoughts and activity in my prayer, that permits your grace to be free and unhampered. So, I can be fully **receptive** to you and expect that you will fill me with your direct communication. And just because I know my lowliness and weakness, there is, finally, no pride or self-confidence to hinder your free gift of yourself. So, in my lowliness I can only be **attentive** to you and wait for you to fill my emptiness.

Chapter 14
The Tranquil Night

John of the Cross completes his treatment of the illuminative way by describing the tranquil night. It seems appropriate for us to end with this topic. Even though the focus of this book is on the **beginning** of contemplation, this one chapter will complete John's spiritual direction regarding the way of progressives. First, let me summarize his entire written teaching that leads up to this final section. Throughout the three books of the *Ascent of Mount Carmel*, John deals with the **active nights** of sense and spirit, which are his development of the purgative way and the preparation for contemplation. Then, in the two books of the *Dark Night*, John treats the **passive nights** of sense and spirit, which develop the illuminative way, especially the beginning of contemplation. Finally, he completes the illuminative way (the way of progressives) in stanzas 13 to 21 of the *Spiritual Canticle* and in some of stanza three of the *Living Flame*.

This latter stage of the illuminative way is still part of the way of progressives.[1] John uses many equivalent terms for this stage of prayer. In the *Ascent of Mount Carmel,* he calls it the **third night**.[2] In the *Spiritual Canticle,* he calls it the **tranquil night**:

> The tranquil night. In this [night]…the soul possesses and relishes all the tranquility, rest and quietude of the peaceful night; and she

---

1 SC, 13, 6.

2 A, I, 2, 5: "…these three nights comprise only one night, a night divided into three parts, just as the natural night. The first night, the night [of the senses]…resembles early evening, that time of twilight when things begin to fade from sight. The second part, faith [the night of the spirit] is completely dark, like midnight. The third part, representing God, is like the very early dawn, just before the break of day." Cf. A, I, 1, 2 and A, II, 2, 1.

receives in God...a fathomless and obscure divine knowledge. As a result, she says that her Beloved is a tranquil night to her.[3]

A very similar term used in this stanza is the **rising dawn,** in order to connect it nicely with the metaphor of the night:

[The soul] very appropriately calls this light "the rising dawn," which means the morning.... This morning light is not clear... but just as the light at the rise of dawn is not entirely night or entirely day, but is...at the break of day, so this divine solitude and tranquility, informed by the divine light, has some share in that light, but not its complete clarity.[4]

Perhaps his favorite term for this stage is that of **spiritual espousal:**

[T]his spiritual flight...in which the soul is placed by God. This state is called spiritual espousal with the Word, the Son of God.... [A] state of peace and delight and gentleness of love begins in her. This state is indicated in these stanzas [14 and 15], in which she [describes] this union of espousal.[5]

Whatever term John uses, there are two elements that make up this stage of prayer:

The soul...finds all the rest and recreation she desires, and understands secrets and strange knowledge of God.... She

---

3   SC, 14-15 (joined as one), 22.
4   *Ibid.* 23.
5   *Ibid.* 2.

tastes…sublimely the wisdom of God…. And above all she understands and enjoys inestimable refreshment of love….[6]

The two elements of the tranquil night are the knowledge and love of God, which result in "rest, recreation, refreshment and love." Notice the similar characteristics mentioned in quotes 3 to 6 above: "quietude, tranquility, peace, delight, gentleness, and recreation." We might even conclude that, for John, these qualities are primary characteristics of this night – which explain his term **tranquil night.**

We should also note that the knowledge and love of God here in the tranquil night are similar, though more advanced, than those we mentioned earlier in chapter 11. Let me quickly recall those four forms of contemplation mentioned there. The first form is a quasi-experiential direct experience of **God's presence**, in which God is experienced without clear understanding or love. The second form is that of an esteem and desire for God, an urgent longing of **love in the will.** Since this love is directly infused by God, it does not require an intellect purified of all natural thoughts. The third form of contemplation is the communication of mystical **knowledge in the intellect**. Sometimes God touches the intellect with divine light and understanding, so that the intellect now understands by means of divine wisdom infused by God. That is, sometimes contemplation communicates mystical knowledge to the intellect while leaving the will in dryness, without the actual union of love. The fourth form of contemplation mentioned is that which acts upon the **intellect and will together**:

Sometimes…contemplation acts upon the intellect and will together and sublimely, tenderly and forcibly enkindles love. …once the intellect is more purged, these two faculties are

---

6   *Ibid.* 14-15 (joined as one), 4.

sometimes united; and in the measure they are both purged, this union becomes so much more perfect and deeper in quality."[7]

In the *Living Flame*, John summarizes these different forms:

> Sometimes ...God...communicates Himself to one faculty more than the other; sometimes more knowledge is experienced than love, and at other times more love than knowledge, and likewise at times all knowledge is felt without love, or all love without any knowledge."[8]

These four forms are present now in the tranquil night, with greater tranquility, refreshment and delight. Even though the experience now increases somewhat in refreshment and clarity, we should not expect it to be completely clear: "This morning light is not clear.... [I]t...has some share in that light, but not its complete clarity."[9]

John also wants us to realize that the experience of this tranquil night varies in different individuals:

> [I]t must not be thought that [God] communicates to all who reach this state...in the same manner and measure of knowledge and feeling. To some souls He gives more and to others less, to some in one way and to others in another, although all alike may be in this state....But the greatest possible communication is recorded here because it includes everything else.[10]

---

7 DN, II, 13, 2.
8 LF, III, 49 (note ftn. 7, p. 23, above).
9 SC, 14-15 (joined as one), 23.
10 *Ibid.* 2.

That is, God treats us individually and differently – perhaps according to our openness and ability to respond. However, John's general treatment will emphasize the most positive experiences of the tranquil night; therefore, he decides to record "the greatest possible communication" that God bestows in this tranquil night.

Even though John is determined to emphasize the most positive aspects of the tranquil night, he deliberately avoids any discussion about rapture, ecstasy and flights of the spirit. In the very beginning of his treatment of the tranquil night, John does mention these experiences, but he spends little time or space in describing them. The reason for this, I suspect, is that throughout his complete works, he is deliberately counteracting the extreme devotionalism and emotional forms of prayer of his day. There was entirely too much value placed on mystical manifestations such as rapture, ecstasy and flight of spirit. John knew these external displays were more likely to mislead than to promote true contemplation. So rather than add to such misleading emotionalism, John was content merely to refer to the writings of his older colleague, St. Teresa of Avila.[11] We will follow John's lead in not emphasizing such phenomena, especially since we are focusing on the earlier stages of contemplation.

What would be more helpful to us now, I believe, is to follow John of the Cross' primary development of the tranquil night as found in the *Spiritual Canticle,* stanzas 13-21. Just before he begins this development, John introduces St. Paul's famous affirmation: "I live, no longer I, but Christ lives in me.... I live by faith in the Son of God who has loved me and given himself up for me"(Gal. 2, 20). He explains:

---

11   SC, 13, 7.

This is the meaning of St. Paul's affirmation.... In saying, I live, now not I, He meant that, even though he had life, it was not his, because he was transformed in Christ.... In accord with this likeness and transformation, we can say that his life and Christ's were **one life through union with him.**[12]

John applies this union and likeness to Christ to those about to begin contemplation. However, he qualifies this likeness to Christ by noting that at this stage, the soul's knowledge, love and following of Christ are imperfect, so that the image of Christ is only **"sketched"** in the soul:

Since the knowledge of [the truths of faith] is imperfect, she says that they are sketched. Just as a sketch is not a perfect painting, so the knowledge of faith is not perfect knowledge.... Over this sketch of faith is drawn in the will of the lover the sketch of love.[13]

So, once the soul has come to this stage of faith and love of Christ, there is an outline of Christ formed in it. John uses this wonderful image of Paul as a way of introducing the next stage of union with Christ in the tranquil night: "The tranquil night/ At the time of the rising of the dawn.../ The supper that refreshes and deepens love."[14] Here, in poetic images, John tells us that the night is almost over. For in this tranquil night, we have some of the morning light of the supernatural knowledge of God and we experience a peace and tranquility in his presence. He continues: "[T]his spiritual flight denotes

---

12   SC, 12, 8 (emphasis added).

13   *Ibid.* 6-7.

14   SC, 14-15, 1.

a high state and union of love, in which after much spiritual exercise, the soul is placed by God. This state is called **spiritual espousal** with the Word, the Son of God."[15] Spiritual espousal seems to be John of the Cross' favorite term for describing this stage. The individual soul is consistently called the bride, and Christ is the bridegroom.[16] In most of John's other works, God is the constant actor mentioned, not Christ. But here in the *Spiritual Canticle,* it is Christ, the Son of God, who is the spouse of the soul. In our day, it would not be surprising to find that this term, spiritual espousal, would sound strange to some people, especially some men. They might prefer terms like **intimate friendship** or loving union with Christ.

Whatever term we prefer, we want to understand what John teaches about the way of becoming intimately united with Christ. Stanzas 20-21 gives a general description:

> In these two stanzas the Bridegroom, the Son of God, gives the bride-soul possession of peace and tranquility by…cleansing it of all its imperfections, bringing under rational control the natural faculties…and quieting all the other appetites…. The Bridegroom…vitally transforms the soul into Himself [so that] all these faculties, appetites and movements lose their natural imperfection and are changed to divine.[17]

That is, Christ completes the work of purification of the soul's natural faculties and appetites, so that it can take the final step of

---

15   *Ibid.* 2.

16   SC, theme before stanza 1: "The beginning of a commentary on the love songs between the bride and Christ, the Bridegroom." Also SC, 14-15, 2; 18, intro. Throughout stanzas 13-21, John constantly speaks of the bride/soul and the Bridegroom/Christ.

17   SC, 20-21 (joined as one), 4.

commitment to him: "The bride must first be a door...that is, she must hold the door of her will open to the Bridegroom that he may enter through the true and complete "yes" of love. This is the **yes of espousal.**"[18] This yes is precisely a profound conformity to the will of God.[19]

The soul becomes the spouse of Christ by its formal and complete conformance to the will of God. John describes the result of this yes of espousal:

> The soul sees and tastes abundance and inestimable riches in this divine union. She finds all the rest and recreation she desires.... She tastes there a splendid spiritual sweetness and gratification, discovers true quiet and divine light.... And above all, she understands and enjoys inestimable refreshment of love which confirms her in love.[20]

Finally, let us finish our study of John of the Cross with an encouraging and important secret. Or, if it is not exactly a secret, it is certainly not adequately reported. That secret is his teaching on the Holy Spirit as the constant guide and source of contemplative prayer. From the very beginning of contemplative prayer, John insists that the **"agent, guide and mover of souls"** is the Holy Spirit. Speaking to spiritual directors about those who have "come to the way of the spirit, which is contemplation," he reminds the spiritual directors that:

> they themselves are not the chief agent, guide and mover of souls in this matter, but that the principal guide is the Holy Spirit, Who

---

18   *Ibid.* 2.
19   *Ibid.* 11.
20   SC, 14-15, 4.

is never neglectful of souls…. [Therefore,] in harmony with the path and spirit along which God leads them, the spiritual director should strive to conduct them into greater solitude, tranquility and freedom of spirit.[21]

Then, in the *Spiritual Canticle,* while commenting on the verse, "Cooled by the breeze of your flight," the Bridegroom "very appropriately terms this love which is caused by the flight a 'breeze' because the Holy Spirit, who is love, is also compared to a breeze in Scripture, for the Holy Spirit is the breath of the Father and the Son."[22] And when the soul encounters spiritual dryness, she should invoke "the Holy Spirit; He it is who will dispel this dryness and sustain and increase her love of the Bridegroom."[23]

Later in the same stanza, John calls the Holy Spirit, "the forerunner" who prepares a dwelling for Christ: "[T]he Bridegroom… sends his Spirit, as he sent his apostles [Lk. 22, 8] to act as his **forerunner,** to prepare his dwelling…. Hence this divine breeze of the Holy Spirit should be greatly desired."[24] Then in stanza 22, John compares the work of the Holy Spirit in preparing the soul for this spiritual union to the **transforming grace** of the Holy Spirit in the apostles at Pentecost.[25] In the *Living Flame,* John similarly speaks of the work of the Holy Spirit in **preparing** the soul for intimate union:

---

21   LF, III, 46 (note ftn. 7, p. 23, above).

22   SC, 13, 11.

23   *Ibid.* 17, 2.

24   *Ibid.* 17, 8-9 (emphasis added). Here I deliberately chose the translation, "forerunner," from the earlier work of E. Allison Peers, because it is more in keeping with the scripture quote cited and makes more sense to me than the translation, "quartermaster," of Kavanaugh and Rodriquez. (See: E. Allison Peers, *The Complete Works of Saint John of the Cross* (Westminster, Maryland: The Newman Press, 1957).

25   *Ibid.* 22, 2.

[D]uring this time of...the anointings of the Holy Spirit, the ointments preparatory for the union with God are more sublime.... [T]hese ointments are a more proximate preparation for union with God...[because] the desire for God is the preparation for union with Him.[26]

The full title of John's last book is the *Living Flame of Love.* Almost the entire book deals with advanced contemplation or the unitive way. (One exception to that theme is paragraphs 30-62 of stanza III, which contains John's guidance for spiritual directors of those beginning contemplation.) At the start of the *Living Flame of Love,* John explains clearly: "This flame of love is the Spirit of the Bridegroom, which is the Holy Spirit.[27] Throughout this entire book, John continues this theme of the **Holy Spirit as the flame of love**.[28] However, I will not develop his teaching about the activity of the Holy Spirit in the unitive way, because our focus remains on the early stages of contemplation. We can conclude that John of the Cross wants us to depend on the infused grace of the Holy Spirit throughout **all the stages of contemplation**. And if we compare what John of the Cross teaches about the work of the Holy Spirit in contemplation to the teaching about the Holy Spirit in St. John's Gospel, we have a wonderful encouragement for our prayer life.

JOHN'S GOSPEL	JOHN OF THE CROSS
"[T]he Father...will give you another **Advocate** to be with	"The chief **agent**...is the Holy Spirit (LF, III, 46).

---

26 LF, III, 26,

27 LF, I, 3.

28 E. g. LF, I, 6; 4, 17.

you always, the Spirit of truth"
(14, 16-17).

"The holy Spirit…will **teach** you everything" (14, 26) and "**guide** you to all truth" (16, 13).	"The principal **guide** is the Holy Spirit" (LF, III, 46).
"[The Spirit will] **remind** you of all that [I] told you" (14, 26) and help you carry it out.	"The chief…**mover** is the Holy Spirit" (LF, III, 46).
"In Johannine thought… **the Paraclete** is given by the risen Jesus precisely as a way **to make permanent his glorified presence** among the disciples, now that his place is with the Father"[29]	"The chief agent, guide and mover of souls [in contemplation] is…the Holy Spirit" (LF, III, 46.)

CHRIST'S UNION WITH THE FATHER AND OUR UNION WITH CHRIST

This tranquil night is a transition to **union with Christ, the Bridegroom**, through the working of the Holy Spirit. Our total union with Christ and transformation into him is the goal of our life in Christ. Jesus himself offers a profound expression of such a transformation in love in the so-called "last Supper Discourse" in John's Gospel. In those five chapters (13-17), Jesus consistently draws paral-

---

29   Raymond Brown, *The Gospel According to John, XIII-XXI*, (NY: Doubleday, 1966), p. 370.

lels between God and himself on the one hand, and himself and us on the other. When Jesus himself describes our intimate union with him, he sometimes describes it conditionally: "If you remain in me"(15, 7), sometimes affirmatively: "whoever believes in me"(14, 12), sometimes urgently: "Remain in me"(15, 4), and sometimes as a goal: "that they also may be in us"(17, 21). The general thrust in all these parallels is that the more we believe in him and love him, the more we are united with Jesus; and our goal is total **transformation in him as he was with the Father,** especially by conformity to God's will. So this wonderful transformation into Jesus himself is included here as both the way and the goal of all our living in Jesus. In that spirit then, we can see the **parallels** that Jesus draws for us.

SUGGESTION FOR PRAYER

▪ Lord Jesus, just as you, even in your humanity, lived entirely transformed into God, your Father, so you invite us to be totally transformed into you.

▪ As you were sent into the world as the complete messenger of your Father, so you send us as your disciples: "As you sent me into the world, so I sent them into the world"(17, 18).

▪ As the words you spoke were entirely the Word of the Father, so the words we speak are yours: "[T]he words you gave to me I have given to them"(17, 8).

▪ Just as your works were those of your Father, so our works are done in you: "The Father who dwells in me is doing his works...[and] whoever believes in me will do the works that I do"(14, 10-12).

- Just as you are entirely dependent on your Father and have no power but his, so we are entirely dependent on you and have no power but yours: "[A] son cannot do anything on his own"(5, 19); and similarly, "[W]ithout me you can do nothing"(15, 5).

- Just as you came down from heaven only "to do…the will of the one who sent me" (6, 38), so we are to keep your commandments as the proof of our love: "Whoever has my commandments and observes them is the one who loves me"(14, 21).

- Just as you and the Father were united in love, so we are united in love with you: "As the Father loves me, so I also love you. Remain in my love"(15, 9).

- Just as you abide in your Father's love, so we are to love others as you loved us: "Just as I…remain in his love…love one another as I love you"(15, 10-12).

- Your union with the Father is our model of union with you: "[A]s you, Father, are in me and I in you, they also may be in us"(17, 21).

- You abide in the Father as we are to abide in you; your life is wholly in God as ours is to be in you: "Remain in me, as I remain in you (15, 4)…as I…remain in his love"(15, 10).

- Without you Lord, we are nothing; when we surrender totally to you and depend on you, we fulfill our whole human life and become transformed in you.

Appendix

IDENTITIES IN JOHN OF THE CROSS

Note: Included under each number are the items that John considers the same or quite similar. The references cited indicate that John considers them identical or similar.

1. Beginners = Meditators = Active Night = Purgative Way.
   A, I, 1, 2-3; 13, 1.

2. Progressives = Contemplatives = Passive Night = Illuminative Way.
   DN, I, 1, 1; 8, 1; 9, 7; 14, 1; DN, II, 1, 2; 3, 3; 23, 10; SC, 22, 3.

3. Perfects = Spiritual Marriage = Divine Union = Unitive Way.
   DN, I, 1, 1; DN, II, 2, 5; SC, theme before 1; 22, 3.

4. Night = Mortification = Privation of desire of all things.
   A, I, 3, 1-4; 11, 1-4; 13, 6-11; A, III, 16, 2-5; 18, 3; 20, 2-3.

5. Dark Night = Emptiness = Detachment from all things = Poverty of spirit.
   A, II, 22, 17; 24, 8.

6. Contemplation = Infused Contemplation = Mystical Theology.
   DN, II, 5, 1; 17, 2.

7. Greater Darkness = Closer to God
    A, II, 3, 4; 4, 6; DN, II, 8, 2-4; 9, 1-5; 16, 1-11.

8. 3 Spiritual Faculties = 3 Faculties of the Soul = Memory,
    Understanding & Will.
    SC, 16, 10; 20 & 21 (as one stanza), 1.

9. Natural Faculties of the Soul = Concupiscible and Irascible
    Faculties.
    SC, 20 & 21 (as one stanza), 4-7.

10. Natural Faculties of the Body = Interior Bodily Senses =
    Imagination & Fantasy
    A, II, 12, 3; SC, 16, 10.

11. Natural Affections = Passions of the Soul = Joy, Hope, Fear &
    Grief.
    A, I, 13, 5; A, III, 16, 2-4; SC, 20 & 21 (as one stanza), 4.

12. Senses of Body = The Exterior Senses = Hearing, Sight, Smell,
    Taste and Touch.
    A, III, 2, 4; 24, 1.

SELECT BIBLIOGRAPHY

Boase, Leonard, S.J., *The Prayer of Faith,* Chicago: Loyola University
Press, 1985.

Burrows, Ruth, *Ascent to Love: The Spiritual Teaching of St. John of
the Cross,* Denville, NJ: Dimension Books, 1987.

_____, *Guidelines for Mystical Prayer,* Denville, NJ: Dimension Books, 1980.

Collins, Ross, O.C.D., *John of the Cross,* Collegeville, MN: Liturgical Press (A Michael Glazier Book), 1990. This is Volume 10 of *The Way of the Christian Mystics,* edited by Noel O'Donoghue, O.C.D.

Dent, Barbara, *My Only Friend is Darkness: Living the Night of Faith,* Notre Dame, IN: Ave Maria Press, 1988.

Dubay, Thomas, S.M., *Fire Within: St. Teresa of Avila, St. John of the Cross, and the Gospel – on Prayer,* San Francisco: Ignatius Press, 1989.

Green, Thomas H., *When the Well Runs Dry, Prayer Beyond the Beginnings,* Notre Dame, IN: Ave Maria Press, 1979.

Jager, Willigis, *Search for the Meaning of Life: Essays and Reflections on the Mystical Experience,* Ligouri, MO: Triumph Books, 1995.

Kavanaugh, Kieran, O.C.D., *John of the Cross, Doctor of Light and Love,* NY: Crossroad Publishing Co., 1999.

Keating, Thomas, *Invitation to Love: The Way of Christian Contemplation,* Rockport, MA: Element, Inc., 1992.

_____, *Open Mind, Open Heart: The Contemplative Dimension of the Gospel,* Rockport, MA: Element, Inc., 1986.

Kinn, James, *Contemplation 2000: St. John of the Cross for Today,* Petersham, MA: St. Bede's Publications, 1997.

Meninger, William A., *The Loving Search for God: Contemplative Prayer and the Cloud of Unknowing,* NY: Continuum, 1994.

Merton, Thomas, *Ascent to Truth,* NY: Harcourt Brace, 1951.

_____, *Contemplative Prayer,* NY: Image Books, 1990.

_____, *The Inner Experience; Notes on Contemplation,* edited by William H. Shannon, NY: Harper Collins Publishers, 2003.

_____, *New Seeds of Contemplation,* NY: New Directions Publishing Corp., 1972.

Muto, Susan, *John of the Cross for Today: The Ascent,* Notre Dame, IN: Ave Maria Press, 1991.

Nemeck. Francis Kelly, O.M.I. and Coombs, Theresa, *Contemplation,* Wilmington DE: Michael Glazier, 1982.

O'Donaghue, Noel, *Mystics for Our Time: Carmelite Meditations for a New Age,* Wilmington, DE: Michael Glazier, 1989.

Payne, Steven, O.C.D. (editor), *John of the Cross,* Washington, DC: Institute of Carmelite Studies, 1992. This is volume 6 of *Carmelite Studies.*

Poulain, A., S.J., *The Graces of Interior Prayer,* London: Routledge and Kegan Paul, Ltd., 1962.

Raguin, Yves, S.J., *Paths to Contemplation,* Wheathampstead, England: Anthony Clark, 1987.

Shannon, William H., *Thomas Merton's Dark Path,* NY: Farrar, Straus, Giroux, 1981.

Underhill, Evelyn, *Mysticism,* NY: Doubleday (Image Books), 1990.

Welch, John, O. Carm., *When Gods Die: An Introduction to John of the Cross,* NY: Paulist Press, 1990.